j920
R12x

D0913194

DETROIT PUBLIC LIBRARY

CHILDREN'S LIBRARY
5201 Woodward
Detroit, MI 48202

DATE DUE

NOV 1 1 1998

SEP 3 0 2000

AET 4623-5
CL

Lives of Notable
Asian Americans

Lives of Notable Asian Americans

BUSINESS ✸ POLITICS ✸ SCIENCE

Angelo Ragaza

EDITORIAL CONSULTANT: RONALD TAKAKI
PROFESSOR OF ETHNIC STUDIES
AT THE UNIVERSITY OF CALIFORNIA, BERKELEY

Chelsea House Publishers

New York Philadelphia

On the cover: Connie Chung, Daniel Inouye, and Dr. David Ho.

Chelsea House Publishers

EDITORIAL DIRECTOR   Richard Rennert
EXECUTIVE MANAGING EDITOR   Karyn Gullen Browne
COPY CHIEF   Robin James
PICTURE EDITOR   Adrian G. Allen
CREATIVE DIRECTOR   Robert Mitchell
ART DIRECTOR   Joan Ferrigno
PRODUCTION DIRECTOR   Sallye Scott

The Asian American Experience

SENIOR EDITOR   Jake Goldberg
SERIES DESIGN   Marjorie Zaum

Staff for *Lives of Notable Asian Americans:*
                    Business ✻ Politics ✻ Science
EDITORIAL ASSISTANT   Scott D. Briggs
PICTURE RESEARCHER   Matthew Dudley

Copyright ©1995 by Chelsea House Publishers, a division of
Main Line Book Co. All rights reserved. Printed and bound in
the United States of America.

First Printing

   3   5   7   9   8   6   4   2

Library of Congress Cataloging-in-Publication Data
Ragaza, Angelo.
Lives of notable Asian Americans: business, politics, science/
Angelo Ragaza.
          p. cm. — (The Asian American experience)
          Includes bibliographical references and index.
Contents: Ellison Onizuka—Subrahmanyan Chandrasekhar—Connie
Chung—Daniel Inouye—David Ho—Josie Natori—Norman Mineta—
Loida Lewis—Chang-Lin Tien—Robert and Doris Matsui—Ieoh
Ming Pei.
ISBN 0-7910-2189-0.
          I. Asian Americans—Biography—Juvenile literature.
          I. Title. II. Series: Asian American experience (New York, N.Y.)
E184.06R34 1995   94–37528
920'.009295—dc20   CIP

CL
11/97

Contents

Ellison Onizuka (1946–1986).

Ellison Onizuka

IN THE 1960S, THE UNITED STATES CELEBRATED A SUCCES-
sion of spectacular triumphs in space. "Space is the new
ocean," President John F. Kennedy had declared, "and this
nation must sail upon it." The Mercury program put the first
Americans in orbit in tiny capsules, which grew larger and
more sophisticated during the subsequent Gemini missions
and Apollo flights. Finally, in July 1969, Neil Armstrong,
Edwin Aldrin, and Michael Collins achieved the inconceivable
and walked on the moon.

In the 1970s, the National Air and Space Administration (NASA) turned its focus to a facility called Skylab, which
would orbit the Earth in space. A 100-ton shuttle vehicle
would transport people and materials from Earth to the space
station and back. Unlike previous spacecraft, which were
launched only once and then fell back to earth, the shuttle,
equipped with wings, would glide back to Earth to be
relaunched again, saving the agency millions of dollars.

In need of pilots and specialists to ride the shuttle,
NASA initiated a nationwide search for new astronauts. The
agency interviewed 8,100 candidates and chose 220 finalists.
Thirty-one-year-old Lieutenant Colonel Ellison Onizuka, an
aerospace engineer at Edwards Air Force Base in California
and a third-generation Japanese American from Hawaii,
impressed the search committee with the quality of his training and experience and with his warm, confident manner. In
1978, NASA selected Ellison to train to become one of the
thirty-five astronauts for the shuttle program. When word got
out, Ellison became an instant star. He and his family back in
Kona, Hawaii, were besieged with phone calls and requests
for interviews.

7

At the Johnson Space Center in Houston, Texas, Ellison and his colleagues studied astronomy, oceanography, computer science, and mathematics. In a simulated weightless environment, they practiced moving and working in space. As a mission specialist, Ellison received training for his specific technical assignments as well as for confidential projects for the U.S. Department of Defense. The astronauts also shared the responsibility of promoting the shuttle program to the American public. They made frequent speeches and public appearances.

In 1982, NASA chose Ellison, along with four other astronauts, for the first manned space shuttle mission. For the first time in the history of manned American space flight, communications about the mission were kept a secret from the press and the public. The date of the mission was repeatedly postponed. Finally, on January 24, 1985, the space shuttle *Discovery* launched from Kennedy Space Center in Florida.

Ellison brought special mementos for the trip—Kona coffee and macadamia nuts from his native Hawaii and a medallion that his father gave him, engraved with a hanging wisteria, the Shin Buddhist crest. He also wore patches from the 442nd Regimental Combat Team and the 100th Battalion, which were made up of Japanese American soldiers who fought during World War II.

The space shuttle *Discovery* completed 48 orbits of the Earth before it returned to Kennedy Space Center three days later, on January 27. Ellison was the first Asian American, the first Japanese American, and the first Buddhist to go into space. For people all around the world, Ellison's triumph belonged to them as well. Ellison Onizuka was a hero.

He was born on June 24, 1946, in Keopu, Hawaii, a village perched 1,500 feet above sea level on the slopes of Mt. Hualalai. His parents, Masamitsu and Mitsue, were Nisei, second-generation Japanese Americans. They farmed the famous coffee that thrived in Kona's cool climate and ran a general store to supply the local farmers.

Ellison was the third of four children. His older sisters, Shirley and Norma, helped their parents in the store and took care of Ellison and his younger brother, Claude. An energetic and curious child, Ellison enjoyed taking things apart to see how they worked. One object that captured his fascination was a roman candle, and one New Year's Eve he shocked his family by setting it off underneath the house.

The Onizukas were a close-knit and supportive family. Ellison also enjoyed the company of many friends. He was bright, hardworking, conscientious, and tempered with an exuberant sense of humor. He was also a stubborn perfectionist. Despite his good nature, he had a temper that could flare whenever he was displeased or if anything stood in the way of his objectives.

As a student, Ellison excelled in math and science. He was committed to helping his community, and in his extracurricular activities he distinguished himself as a leader. He was a member of the National Honor Society. In his Boy Scout troup he earned the rank of Eagle Scout. He was a member of the Young Buddhist Association and the 4-H Club and eventually became the statewide president of both. Ellison

The ill-fated crew of the space shuttle Challenger, *flight 51-L. Mission specialist Onizuka stands in the back row on the far left, next to schoolteacher S. Christa McAuliffe.*

was also an accomplished athlete. He enjoyed basketball and baseball, and he played center field in the 1962 and 1964 Big Island North Division championship teams.

Besides his schoolwork and extracurricular activities, Ellison helped his family in the store. During the summer and fall he picked coffee beans in the family's fields. He also held part-time jobs as a baggage handler for Aloha Airlines and as an employee of a trucking company, making deliveries in the Kona area.

In 1964, Ellison graduated from Konawaena High School with honors. Before he graduated, he decided he wanted to become an aerospace engineer. He applied to college at the Air Force Academy but was rejected. Making his first trip to the mainland, he enrolled instead at the University of Colorado at Boulder, with a 4-H scholarship in hand.

In college he devoted himself to his course work and joined the Air Force Reserve Officers Training Program (ROTC) at school. He spent winter vacations learning how to ski, an exotic sport for a native Hawaiian. He returned to Hawaii during the summers to spend time with his family in Keopu. During his senior year, he met Lorna Leiko Yoshida, a student at Colorado State College (now known as the University of Northern Colorado). Lorna and Ellison found that they had a lot in common. Like Ellison, Lorna was Sansei (third-generation Japanese American), Hawaiian, and Buddhist. Both were active in clubs and organizations on campus. Lorna's initial suspicions that the studious Ellison was square were soon dispelled. She found Ellison to be great fun at parties, and he loved to play practical jokes. Ellison and Lorna married the day after Ellison graduated, in June 1969, with Ellison's mother present.

Before graduation, however, the Onizuka family mourned a tragic loss. In February, Ellison's father, Masumitsu, suffered a fatal heart attack. Ellison and his father had been very close. As the oldest son, Ellison's first impulse was to leave Boulder and return to Hawaii permanently to replace Masumitsu as the head of the family. But Mitsue Onizuka persuaded her son that the family would be fine, and that Masumitsu would have wanted his son to continue his education. Ellison went back to school with even greater determination to succeed.

In October, Lorna gave birth to their first daughter, Janelle. By December, Ellison had earned a master's degree in aerospace engineering from the University of Colorado, and he graduated from the ROTC program with the rank of second lieutenant. The following month, in January 1970, Ellison joined the U.S. Air Force. For the next four years, he worked at McClellan Air Force Base in Sacramento, California as an aerospace flight test engineer. He engineered and tested aircraft safety systems for numerous military aircraft, including the F-84, F-100, F-105, F-111, EC-121T, T-33, T-39, T-28, and the A-1. Ellison was then admitted to the Air Force Test Pilot School at Edwards Air Force Base in the Mojave Desert, California. From August 1974 to July 1975, he learned how to fly aircraft, and he tested the functioning of new aircraft systems while in flight. While he attended pilot school, Ellison and Lorna's second daughter, Darien, was born in March 1975.

After completing the test pilot program, Ellison served on the school staff, first as squadron flight test engineer and then in the training resources branch as chief of the engineering support section.

In 1978, Ellison was selected to train for the space shuttle program. His new responsibilities were complex and time consuming. Eighty-hour work weeks were a strain on the family, leaving Lorna to run the household and care for the children alone. But Ellison remained devoted to his family. He jogged in the early morning with his daughters and tutored them in math. Janelle and Darien also played on their school's soccer team. Ellison, an officer of the soccer booster club, cheered his daughters at soccer matches.

After the successful flight of the *Discovery* in 1985, Ellison was once more thrust into the limelight. When he returned to Hawaii, he was given a hero's welcome and hounded by the media. He embarked on an exhausting tour involving public appearances, state dinners and banquets, parades, and countless speaking engagements. He never let fatigue slow him down. He talked about his seventy-three hours in space with rapture, and often was at a loss for words to describe the beauty of Earth when seen from space. "It's a beautiful planet," he later said, "It is the most beautiful sight you'll ever see, something that film just can't capture."

"When dad first came down, I never heard the end of him talking about space," his daughter Janelle said, "He told me it wasn't always dark up there—sometimes it was a bright

white . . . the sky was sometimes even orange and yellow." Nor did Ellison leave his sense of humor on the ground. While in the gravity-free environment of the shuttle, Janelle said, "He experimented with the macadamia nuts, putting them in the air and trying to eat them."

Ellison did most of his speaking at schools because he loved children and was eager to share his experience in space travel with them. In his talks he encouraged young people to pursue their dreams, and to surpass the limits perceived by generations before them. "El worked real hard to leave something for the yonsei [fourth-generation Japanese Americans]," Lorna Onizuka later told an interviewer, "like the nisei [second-generation Japanese Americans] had left him."

Ellison also returned to Kona and visited his proud family and friends. Those who knew Ellison well remarked that even after his space flight, he was still a country boy from Kona with his feet on the ground, ever faithful to his roots. He traveled to Japan, where he made a pilgrimage to his

Ellison Onizuka addresses a small gathering after the arrival of the Challenger *crew at the Kennedy Space Center at Cape Canaveral, Florida, on January 23, 1986, five days before the fatal flight.*

13

Enroute to the launchpad just hours before the flight are Onizuka, McAuliffe, and other members of 51-L's flight crew.

family's ancestral village and gave presentations about space travel.

In 1985, Onizuka received the news that he was chosen for the seven-person crew of the space shuttle *Challenger.* The flight was slated to take place in January 1986. This time news of the mission was globally publicized and sparked the imagination of millions of Americans. The crew was diverse and included men and women from seven different states, of six different faiths, and three ethnic groups.

On the morning of January 28, 1986, thousands of visitors from around the United States, including families and schoolchildren, gathered on the grounds of the Kennedy Space Center, awaiting the launch of the space shuttle *Challenger* with excitement and anticipation. At 11:38 A.M., the *Challenger* launched. But seventy-three seconds later, one of the rocket boosters that lifted the shuttle into space malfunctioned. The *Challenger* exploded in the sky, taking Ellison's life along with those of the other crew-members—Ron McNair, Dick Scobee, Michael Smith, Judith Resnik, Greg Jarvis, and Christa McAuliffe.

On June 2, Ellison's remains were buried at a cemetery in Oahu, amid the stunning beauty of the Punchbowl Crater. Since then, visitors have arrived daily in droves to pay tribute to him and to refresh the leis on his grave. The cemetery is the most visited site in Hawaii, and it is also the most visited military cemetery in the United States. There, Ellison's grave is surrounded by the graves of military heroes, including the very Japanese American soldiers to whose memories he paid special tribute on his first flight into space. Many of the 2,403 Americans who were killed in the attack on Pearl Harbor were also among the first to be buried in Punchbowl Cemetery.

Every Memorial Day, schoolchildren throughout Hawaii sew leis, and hundreds of boyscouts come to the cemetery to place two of the leis on each grave, along with an American flag. Sixty percent of the visitors who come to pay tribute to American veterans are from Japan.

After his death, Hawaiians organized quickly to commemorate their homegrown hero. The space observatory of the University of Hawaii, perched halfway up the slopes of Hawaii's highest mountain, the 13,796-foot-high Mauna Kea, was renamed the Onizuka International Center of Astronomy. The airport at Kona was renamed the Ellison Onizuka Airport. Across the Pacific, in Los Angeles, the city council ordained that Weller Street in the district known as Little Tokyo be renamed Lt. Col. Ellison S. Onizuka Street.

Ellison's brother, Claude, and other community leaders organized to form the Onizuka Memorial Committee, with the aim of establishing an institution that would commemorate Ellison Onizuka and the messages he wished to communicate to youth. On July 21, 1991, over five years after Ellison's death, the Ellison Onizuka Space Center opened at the airport in Kona. The center, built with $2 million provided by the state and the memorial committee, houses fourteen exhibits geared to educate young people about aerospace and aerospace technology. Its exhibits are updated periodically as technology in the space program changes.

At the museum there are mementos of Ellison, including a bronze bust and his space suit. On one wall are inscribed his words. He believed that everything was possible, and he urged youth to follow their dreams. "Your vision is not limited by what your eye can see," the inscription reads, "but by what your mind can imagine."

for models, for elegance and meaning in nature, to which Chandra has devoted his life.

Chandra was born in India and educated in England, but for most of his professional career he has lived in the United States. To leave India has been considered by Indians to be immoral, an act of betrayal. But Chandra's accomplishments, like those of Indian scientists such as Meghnad Saha, S. N. Bose, and C. V. Raman, ultimately brought glory to India and demonstrated the magnitude of Indian talent before the world, just as India struggled for its independence from Britain and took its first steps as an independent nation.

Chandra's ancestors were Brahmans. In Sanskrit, "Brahmana" means "possessors of sacred knowledge." Among the various social classes of Hindu India, which included warriors, traders, and menial workers, Brahmans—the priests—held the highest rank. They performed religious ceremonies, and because they held exclusive rights to study and recite sacred texts, Brahmans controlled knowledge and scholarship in India for centuries. During British rule, which lasted from 1852 until 1947, many Brahmans held positions as civil servants. As the most educated Indians, they were the first to be exposed to European literature, art, and science.

Chandra was born into an unconventional, highly distinguished family. His grandfather, Ramanathan Chandrasekhar, an educator and an agnostic, was a devotee of English literature and philosophy as well as mathematics and physics. Chandra's uncle, C. V. Raman, was a physicist of international fame who won the 1930 Nobel Prize in Physics and was responsible for promoting the study of the physical sciences in India. Chandra's father, C. S. Ayyar, was a chief auditor for British railway companies who in his spare time played the violin and wrote books about music, as well as some fiction. In 1909, he was posted to Lahore, Pakistan. Chandra was born there on October 19, 1910. Chandra's large family included, aside from himself, six sisters and three brothers. He was the third child and the first son. When he was eight, his father was transferred to Madras, a large city on the eastern coast of the Bay of Bengal.

Chandra's education began when he was five, on an important Hindu festival day, when he sat next to his father and wrote three letters of the Tamil alphabet in the sand. Until he went to high school, Chandra was educated at home by his parents. It was a common practice among middle-class families in India who wished to avoid sending their children to the poorly run public schools but did not enjoy the privilege of sending their children to private schools, which were reserved for British children and for the children of Indian royal families. In the mornings before Chandra's father left for work, he taught the children English and math. In the afternoon, Chandra's mother taught the children Tamil and supervised their language lessons. Chandra showed an early affinity for English and math. He jumped ahead of the assignments and studied math books on his own. He was fortunate to have access to a large reading library left to the family by Chandra's grandfather. When the family moved to Madras, C. S., realizing that in his oldest son he had something of a child prodigy on his hands, hired private tutors to teach Chandra. When Chandra was eleven, he skipped two years of high school and was accepted directly into the third year at the Hindu High School in Triplicane, Madras.

Before high school, Chandra had enjoyed the freedom to study his favorite subjects. But in high school, he was also required to study history, geography, and science. At first Chandra was disappointed in the curriculum. But the fourth-year curriculum, which included algebra and geometry, stimulated his interest anew. Outside of class, he delved into calculus and physics on his own. Chandra finished high school and entered Presidency College in Madras at the age of fifteen.

Thanks to C. S. Ayyar's work, the family enjoyed a comfortable life. Household help freed them from performing daily chores, and C. S.'s position with the railways enabled the family to travel throughout India, a privilege enjoyed by very few Indians. Since his father traveled often, Chandra's mother, Sitalakshmi, supervised the household and reared the children. She made a point of steeping them in their Hindu heritage and read aloud to them every morning from the *Ramayana,* which, along with the *Mahabharata,* is one of India's greatest epic poems. His mother also introduced Chandra to the work of the Swedish playwright Henrik Ibsen. An accomplished scholar herself, Sitalakshmi translated one of Ibsen's plays, *A Doll's House,* into Tamil.

As a youth, Chandra was considerate and caring. Despite his performance at school, his warm character stemmed any impulse toward envy or competitiveness among his siblings and classmates. That his parents, like most traditional Indian parents, considered the education of his sisters less important than his own and that of his younger brothers, saddened him. Rather than receiving private tutoring, his sisters were sent to public school. Chandra found it unjust that his two older sisters had to stop going to school while they were still in their early teens because they were getting married.

C. S. was a traditional father, authoritative and aloof, and he demanded obedience from everyone. His ambitions for Chandra's future—to take the civil service exam and become a civil servant—were respectable by conventional standards, but far less interesting than Chandra's own ambitions. Chandra was struck by the internationally recognized achievements of the great mathematician Srinivasa Ramanujan, as well as those of his own uncle. While Chandra was a teenager, he decided to become a scientist. At Presidency College in Madras he studied physics, chemistry, English, and Sanskrit, but he was most fond of physics and English. He wanted to take the B.A. honors degree in math, but his father, who wanted him to study physics, stopped him. Chandra had no intention of pursuing his father's lackluster ambitions for his future, but he did acquiesce to his father's desire for him to study physics, and he completed all the requirements for the

Chandrasekhar at the University of Chicago in 1939. He was 29 years old.

physics course with distinction. But this did not prevent him from attending mathematics lectures on his own. As a student, Chandra was well-rounded. Aside from being an outstanding scholar, he played tennis, competed in track and field events, and was a good debater.

In 1928, when Chandra was 18, his uncle Raman made an important discovery about the molecular scattering of light that would later be known as the Raman effect. Chandra went to Calcutta for the summer to work in his uncle's laboratory, but his debut in experimental work was a failure; within his first week, he broke an important piece of equipment. However, it was an exhilarating time for his uncle and for the future of science in India. Chandra was happy to be part of the environment, absorbing the enthusiasm of Raman and his colleagues.

Chandra returned to Madras to begin his second year of study. Arnold Sommerfeld, a well-known German physicist who visited Madras and met with Chandra, suggested that Chandra study developments in atomic theory, including the new theory of quantum statistics. On the basis of his studies, Chandra wrote a paper called "The Compton Scattering and the New Statistics." In 1929, he sent the paper to Ralph Howard Fowler, an astrophysicist in England, and with some minor changes the paper was published in the Proceedings of the Royal Society later that year. Chandra also presented his findings to the Indian Science Congress. The audience, stunned to discover that Chandra was only 18 years old and that he had written the paper entirely on his own, launched the young scientist's career with a thunderous ovation.

While Chandra was in college, the Indian nationalist movement was gaining momentum. Chandra, who had experienced British racism, supported the movement. To protest the domination of the school curriculum by the British view of history, which totally neglected Indian history, Chandra intentionally submitted a bad history paper. He joined the throngs of students who took to the streets of Madras to welcome Jawaharlal Nehru, the head of Gandhi's Congress Party, even though the principal of the school, an Englishman, had expressly forbidden the students to do so.

Despite his insubordination, the principal called Chandra into his office in 1930 to announce that Chandra had been awarded an Indian government scholarship to study in England. Chandra was thrilled, but two problems faced him: his mother's failing health, and strong disapproval from friends and family over his leaving India. Nevertheless, Chandra's mother, who had always been supportive of Chandra's interests (often at variance with Chandra's father), urged him to accept the opportunity. He left Madras for England on July 22, 1930, accompanied to the boat by family, teachers, and friends, who gathered to wish him great success.

Rather than taking part in the social activities and festivities on the ship, Chandra immersed himself in his studies. In the course of his thoughts, he began to doubt the current theory that all stars, as they age, become white dwarfs—small, highly dense stars that burn brightly until they flicker out as stellar ash. Using Einstein's theory of relativity and the new quantum mechanics, Chandra found that if the mass of a star was greater than a certain critical mass—perhaps three times as massive as our Sun—the star would not become a white dwarf. It would continue to collapse under extreme gravitational forces, producing new states of superdense matter. Years would pass before this discovery, which Chandra

23

made at the age of 19, would be acknowledged as one of the most important scientific discoveries of the century. It would lead to the discoveries of pulsars, that is, neutron stars, and black holes.

Chandra arrived in London on August 19, and when he got to Cambridge, he lost no time in finding comfortable lodgings. Despite the change in cuisine, he adhered strictly to his vegetarian diet, as he would continue to do for the rest of his life. But he found life at Cambridge to be somewhat lonely and anonymous. In India, he had been respected and well known. In England, he was just another student.

He soon settled into a brisk schedule of physics lectures. In his own time he sharpened his mathematical skills to bring them up to par with his knowledge of physics. Chandra came into close contact with many famous scientists, including Arthur Eddington and Edward Milne. During Chandra's first year, he was introduced to the Royal Astronomical Society in London and began to attend their meetings, which took place every second Friday of the month, and at which Chandra began to contribute papers and present his work.

As he neared the end of his first year at Cambridge, Chandra received the tragic news that his mother had died. He became depressed. His unhappiness with the progress of his work at Cambridge was growing; as a theoretical astrophysicist, he was an outsider. His research problems were outside the central sphere of scientific interest at Cambridge, which lay more squarely in the realm of subatomic physics. Because of this, Chandra toyed with the idea of pursuing pure physics rather than astrophysics. To this end, the physicist Paul Dirac urged Chandra to go to Copenhagen to study with

Niels Bohr. After securing permission from the Indian government, Chandra left for Denmark in August 1932.

Chandra devoted most of the two to three weeks between academic terms to the study of literature. He was especially fond of Russian literature, and he read English translations of the works of Turgenev, Chekhov, Dostoevsky, and Tolstoy. Among English writers he enjoyed Virginia Woolf, T. S. Eliot, Thomas Hardy, John Galsworthy, and Bernard Shaw. From graduate school on, he devoted a month out of every summer to the study of literature, until the demands of science made this impossible.

In contrast to Cambridge, which was dominated by the English and where the academic climate was chilly and unwelcoming, the atmosphere at the Institute for Theoretical Physics in Copenhagen, whose scientists came from countries all around the world, was truly international and friendly. At Cambridge, Chandra had experienced loneliness and a sense of being an outsider; in Copenhagen, his colleagues were warm and supportive, and Chandra finally felt a sense of belonging. While he was there, he completed more papers, and in February 1933 he went to Belgium to deliver a series of lectures about stellar atmospheres and the internal makeup of stars. For his well-received lectures he was awarded a bronze medal, and eventually the lectures were published as a book. His success in Belgium helped to clarify Chandra's desire to work as an astrophysicist.

He returned to Cambridge in May 1933, with more material than he needed for his thesis, and he gave up his plan to abandon astrophysics for pure physics. Chandra prepared his thesis for defense and began to plan for the future. The Indian government scholarship would expire in August 1933,

*Professor Chandrasekhar
receives his Nobel Prize in
Stockholm from Sweden's
King Carl Gustaf. He
shared that year's physics
prize with William
Fowler of the California
Institute of Technology.*

and the terms of the scholarship required Chandra to return to India to work and teach. But the scientific climate in India, riddled with bureaucracy, petty rivalry, and favoritism, was not one in which Chandra wanted to conduct his research.

He successfully defended his thesis before Eddington and Fowler on June 20 and then wrote to the Indian government to request an extension of his scholarship for one year. The request was summarily rejected. Chandra learned of another way he could stay at Cambridge: if he could win one of the highly coveted Trinity College fellowships, which would provide free rooms, dining privileges, and a stipend for four years. But he was warned that the competition was very stiff and that his chances of winning were extremely slim. He applied anyway. He was in the midst of preparing to leave Cambridge to stay with Milne at Oxford when he found out that he had beaten the odds and had been selected.

As a fellow, Chandra began to feel more confident about his decision to continue in astrophysics. He began to enjoy himself. He made more friends on campus and he established better relations with individual members of the scientific community at Cambridge. On Sundays he took long, 18 to 20 mile walks to visit towns nearby. In the summer of

1934, Chandra visited the Soviet Union and delivered lectures in Leningrad (now St. Petersburg) and Moscow.

Along with his research, Chandra continued his activities with the Royal Astronomical Society. The prestige of holding a Trinity fellowship simplified Chandra's admission as a fellow to the Society. In his first presentation to the Society in June 1933, Chandra read a half dozen papers, all of which were well received and published. In a paper that Chandra submitted to the January 1935 meeting of the Royal Astronomical Society, he elaborated upon the discovery about white dwarfs which he had made six years before, on the long boat journey from Bombay to England. Chandra's ideas were controversial. Arthur Eddington, who had pioneered research into stellar interiors and was the first physicist to promote Einstein's theory of relativity in the English language, was present at Chandra's thesis defense and was familiar with Chandra's work. Standing fast in his conviction that all stars became white dwarfs, Eddington ridiculed Chandra's findings, dismissed his calculations, and belittled his reasoning, humiliating him before the entire astronomical community. There was little an obscure young scientist like Chandra could do to defend himself against the criticisms of an established authority like Eddington.

Instead of fighting Eddington as most scientists would have done, Chandra summarized his findings in his first book, *An Introduction to the Study of Stellar Structure* (1939), and withdrew from the debate. But time and science were on his side. Three decades later, the "Chandrasekhar limit," which defines how massive a star has to be to collapse beyond the white dwarf stage, has become a standard term in the astrophysical vocabulary. Five decades later, Chandra received the Nobel Prize for the discovery.

After the controversy with Eddington, Chandra turned to a new area of research, stellar dynamics. After a few years of work in that field, he published his findings in a second book entitled *Principles of Stellar Dynamics* (1943). This pattern of identifying a new research problem, working intensely on it for several years, and then publishing his findings, repeated itself numerous times throughout Chandra's career.

After his first year as a Trinity fellow, Harvard invited Chandra to lecture for a few months. Little did he realize that the invitation would change his life. Back in India, Chandra's father pleaded with Chandra to return, marry, accept a job offer, and settle down. But Chandra decided to accept the invitation to Harvard. He left England for the United States on November 30, 1935. Unlike his first long ocean voyage, Chandra used the time to put science aside and return to his love of literature. As the ship crossed the Atlantic, he read all the plays of Henrik Ibsen.

Chandra found university life in America to be very different from his experience at Cambridge. There were no caps and gowns, no formal dinners, and the atmosphere was informal, relaxed, and friendly. He quickly befriended the other astronomers at Harvard. Noting the popularity of his lectures, Harvard offered him the chance to stay longer with a fellowship that would provide rooms, dinner, and a stipend, along with the chance to conduct his research with complete freedom. At the same time, Chandra received a competing offer of a research associate position at the University of Chicago. Chandra visited Chicago's Yerkes Observatory in Wisconsin. He was impressed by the observatory's placid natural setting, and he saw in it an environment in which he could finally work in peace. On his way back to England, he decided to accept the offer from Chicago. He sought the counsel of his advisers at Cambridge, and they approved of his decision. In spite of the obvious desire of American universities to recruit him, no one at Cambridge came forward with a competing offer. At the time, there was still widespread prejudice in England against offering permanent university positions to Indians.

In July 1936, Chandra returned briefly to India. Six years had passed since he had left. He returned to Chandra Vilas and reunited with his family, as well as with a young woman named Lalitha Doraiswamy, whom he had met while they were students in the honors physics course at Presidency College. Lalitha's family lived adjacent to the Chandrasekhars. The two young people had been attracted to each other in college, but bashfulness and awkwardness inhibited both from revealing their feelings. After Chandra had gone to England, they kept in touch through letters. With time, their feelings for each other deepened, and in their letters they began to discuss making a future together.

Lalitha was an unconventional Indian woman. Her family considered education as important for girls as it was for boys, and unlike Chandra's sisters, Lalitha and her sisters were barred from marrying while they were still in their teens. Lalitha's two older sisters studied medicine and became doctors, and her younger sister earned a master's degree in Sanskrit. Lalitha earned her master's degree in physics, and it was no small boon to Chandra that she shared his scientific interests. While Chandra was in Cambridge, Lalitha sought to pursue her interest in physics, but she got no help or encouragement from anyone at Presidency College. She expressed an interest in going to England to do research, but her mother refused to allow her to go alone. Lalitha taught high school and middle school for a while before she returned to Presidency College and then visited the Indian Institute of Science in Bangalore with hopes of continuing her research in physics. But no one at these institutions could assign her a meaningful problem. While she waited for Chandra to return to India, she studied on her own.

They married on September 11, 1936. Theirs was a rare marriage, for it was not arranged. There was a one-day ceremony at a Hindu temple that bypassed many of the traditional wedding formalities, including the matching of their horoscopes, the exchange of a dowry, and the customary four-day ceremony. The two sailed for England on October 13, 1936, and then to Boston on December 5, from which they headed to the Yerkes Observatory at Williams Bay. Once settled into their home, Chandra immersed himself in his work, and Lalitha managed the household and got involved in local women's organizations. Williams Bay became their home for the next twenty-seven years.

Chandra's research over the course of several decades encompassed seven phases: stellar structure (1929–1939); stellar dynamics (1938–1943); radiative transfer, the illumination and polarization of the sunlit sky, planetary and stellar atmospheres, and the quantum theory of the negative ion of hydrogen (1943–1950); hydrodynamic and hydromagnetic stability (1952–1961); the equilibrium and stability of ellipsoidal figures (1961–1968); the general theory of relativity and relativistic astrophysics (1962–1971); and the mathematical theory of black holes (1974–1983). In each of these areas of research, he produced many papers, followed by a definitive book meticulously detailed, thorough, and clearly written. (An article published in a German newspaper once boasted that if all the formulas, equations, and text in Chandra's publications were put end to end, they would cover the distance between the Earth and the Moon!)

During the 1940s, Chandra followed the events in India with dismay. All of the leaders of the nationalist movement were jailed and strikes and riots had broken out across the country. As the United States entered the war in Europe, Chandra was asked to contribute his expertise to military research in the ballistics laboratory at the Aberdeen Proving Grounds in Maryland. From February to December 1943, Chandra commuted between Williams Bay and the APG. He was glad to see his knowledge applied practically in Aberdeen. But while he was there he frequently experienced racial discrimination of the crassest kind. He was repeatedly refused service in the officers' mess until it was made clear that he was one of the research scientists on the compound. Once, while he was waiting to be let in at the gate, the man at the entrance cried, "Eh, blackie, there, you just wait until I come!" It is easy to understand why Chandra avoided bringing Lalitha to Aberdeen.

In 1942, Chandra was promoted to an associate professorship at the University of Chicago, and he became a full professor in 1943. Competing offers arrived from other universities, but he turned them down to remain at Chicago, for he was happy there. He taught at least six courses a year on stellar interiors, stellar atmospheres, and stellar dynamics. His research continued apace. But in the early 1950s, his activities were disrupted and frustration returned. In 1952, he

became the managing editor of the *Astrophysical Journal,* the
most important journal of its kind in the world. His responsibilities as editor were intense, time consuming, and often
tedious. He had to coordinate communications between
scientists, some of them recalcitrant and uncooperative, at
research universities around the world. Chandra edited the
journal for 19 years. In addition, the curriculum of Chicago's
astronomy department was revised to emphasize observa-
tional astronomy rather than theoretical astrophysics. Chandra's courses were, in effect, phased out. He accepted an
invitation to join the physics department, where his lectures
proved to be very popular. Even though he had been appointed
to the astronomy department, Chandra continued to teach in
the physics department.

Later, Chandra realized that the humiliation of having
his courses canceled was part of a larger pattern of unfair, even
discriminatory treatment at Chicago. Chandra's colleagues at
Yerkes were promoted to tenure and given salary raises four
years earlier than he, even though they had the same qualifications. From the time Chandra's colleagues arrived at Yerkes,
secretaries assisted them. Chandra did not have a secretary
until 1944. It wasn't until the early 1960s that the former
president of the university, Robert Hutchins, made a stunning
disclosure. He revealed that while the University of Chicago
considered Chandra among the candidates for the posts at
Yerkes in the 1930s, Henry Gale, dean of the physical sciences, did not want Chandra on campus because Chandra was
not white. Hutchins had intervened, and he personally offered
the position to Chandra.

Raman had warned Chandra and Lalitha about the
discriminatory treatment he had experienced in the United

States. In several instances, one in which they were refused a hotel room during a visit to New York, Chandra and Lalitha experienced American racism firsthand. But this did not dispel their hope in the country, or their desire to become more fully a part of it. In 1953, despite the strong disappoval of family and friends in India, Chandra and Lalitha became U.S. citizens. When they first arrived, they had no intentions of remaining permanently. Indeed, U.S. immigration law made it impossible for them to do so, since the Exclusion Law barred Asians from becoming citizens. Chandra had professional motives for becoming a citizen, because his status as a noncitizen constantly complicated his ability to carry out his administrative duties at the university. During a visit to India in 1951, Chandra and Lalitha finally realized the extent to which they had come to feel at home in the United States, and they saw that their chances of ever returning to India were remote.

Moreover, they were fascinated by the energy of the American political climate at the time. They were attracted to Adlai Stevenson, the 1952 Democratic candidate for president, because his message of hope and optimism for the United States spoke to Chandra and Lalitha's desire to stay in the country. Even though they were not citizens, they joined the local Democratic party; Lalitha went to meetings and helped to raise funds for Stevenson. But the Chandrasekhars' status as noncitizens hindered them from becoming more deeply involved in American political life. In December 1952, however, the new Immigration and Naturalization Act made it possible for a small quota of Asians to become citizens. Chandra and Lalitha took a citizenship course to study American history and the U.S. constitution, and in October 1953

they became citizens. In 1960, they were active on behalf of
John F. Kennedy's presidential campaign.

In 1962, Chandra and Lalitha visited India again.
This time they remained for six months as Chandra toured
the country giving lectures. Chandra also met with Prime
Minister Nehru. In 1968, he was again in India to deliver the
Nehru memorial lecture, and during several meetings on that
visit with Prime Minister Indira Gandhi, Chandra was
strongly impressed by her competence, courage, and strength.

Chandra and Lalitha continued to live in Williams
Bay until 1964, when they moved to Chicago. On the University of Chicago's main campus, Chandra's legend continued to grow. In the classroom he was a serious, magnetic
presence. He was always immaculately dressed, and he spoke
in the elegant, cadenced English of an earlier era. His enthusiasm for his subject matter was infectious, and he delivered
his insights with style and power.

Students were attracted to him but intimidated by
him. However, Chandra always considered teaching a vital
part of his vocation, having advised over 50 students in
doctoral programs. For instance, in 1943, he had driven eight
hundred miles between Williams Bay, Wisconsin, and the
Aberdeen Proving Grounds in Maryland once a week to teach
a class of two students, Tsung Dao Lee and Chen Ning Yang,
both of whom went on to win the Nobel Prize in physics in
1957.

In 1980, Chandra retired from teaching, but he continued his research and writing. In 1981, he visited Russia a
second time, his first visit in forty-seven years. In 1983, he
published a groundbreaking book on the theory of black

Chandrasekhar and his wife, Lilitha, take a morning stroll across the campus of the University of Chicago.

holes. Along with his prodigious research, Chandra's output as a writer has been prolific. His books have become classics in their fields, and his prose has been universally praised for its clarity and elegance. Chandra attributes this to his deep love of literature, to which he has returned time and again throughout his life. In 1974, while he recuperated from a heart attack and a bypass operation, he read all the plays of Shakespeare.

Between science and art, Chandra has always seen close parallels. Both pursuits seek to unravel the mysteries of life, both follow the eternal human quest for meaning, understanding, and beauty. In the speech he gave to accept the Nobel Prize, he expressed his gratitude for the encouragement the award offered to people like himself, who faithfully followed the path of discovery in a long and lonely search for truth. "The simple is the seal of the true," he said, "and beauty is the splendor of truth."

Constance (Connie) Yu-Hwa Chung.

FOR MILLIONS OF AMERICANS, CONNIE CHUNG'S NAME IS a household word. Her achievements as a broadcast journalist for over two decades have earned her three Emmy awards, one of the highest salaries in television, and a place among the ranks of America's prime-time icons: Barbara Walters, Diane Sawyer, Walter Cronkite, Peter Jennings, Tom Brokaw, and Dan Rather. Before she was chosen to coanchor the "CBS Evening News" with Dan Rather, the makeup of America's national news anchorship had been invariably middle-aged, male, and white. That changed for a brief spell from 1976 to 1978, when Barbara Walters coanchored the "ABC Nightly News" with Harry Reasoner (it was a brief experiment, for the two did not get along.)

It seemed that there would be no new faces on the horizon until 1989, the year that Connie Chung returned to CBS from NBC and began to anchor the "Evening News" on Sunday and substitute for Dan Rather whenever he was absent. Chung's warmth and vitality struck a chord with television viewers across the country, who were accustomed to Rather's steady but dry delivery of the day's news. CBS affiliates, noting the response in their ratings, clamored for more frequent Chung appearances. Finally on June 1, 1993, Connie Chung made her highly publicized debut as the show's coanchor.

Constance Yu-Hwa Chung was born in 1946, the tenth and last child of William and Margaret Chung, and the only child to be born in the United States. Three sons and two daughters died before the Chungs, with their four surviving daughters—Josephine, Charlotte, June, and Mimi—fled China in 1945 and arrived in the United States.

Constance (Connie) Yu-Hwa Chung

37

William and Margaret were by most measures a traditional Chinese couple. They met on the day of their wedding in Suzhou, China, when they were both still teenagers. William, an intelligence officer for Chinese Nationalist leader Chiang Kai-shek, kept concubines, a common practice among many Chinese men that nonetheless infuriated Margaret. She was relieved that the practice was brought to a halt once the Chungs settled in the United States.

The fact that their tenth child was a girl must have deeply disappointed William, scion of a culture that deeply valued sons over daughters. Connie must have sensed this regret early in her life, for she soon decided that she wanted to live her life as a son, perpetuating the family and bringing honor to the family name. Her status as the youngest, and therefore least authoritative, member of the family may have also driven her desire for recognition. Her mother and her older sisters were always more lively, outspoken, and assertive than she. Despite her phenomenal success, Connie has not outgrown her status as baby of the family. She still defers to her mother's requests to perform basic chores whenever the Chungs get together.

Connie's ascent to the summit of broadcast journalism was steady and took over two decades. She graduated from the University of Maryland in 1969 with a degree in journalism. Shortly thereafter, she got a job at WTTG-TV, a local CBS news affiliate in Washington, as a copy person (a glorified title for a station receptionist). Eventually she took a job as a newsroom secretary and waited to apply for a position that would use her journalism skills. When a place on the newswriting staff opened, she applied for it. But her superiors told her that she would be more valuable to the office if she

remained a secretary. Connie's response quickly dispelled any notion that she would accept the Asian female stereotype of self-effacing obedience. She marched across the street and offered a bank teller her job. It became clear to management that Connie's determination to report the news was unshakable. The teller got Connie's job, and Connie was promoted to the position of newswriter.

In 1971, Connie went on the air as a reporter for the first time. Her beat was hard political news, and she covered the most momentous events of that time, including Senator

Anchorwoman Connie Chung in her office in the NBC headquarters building at 30 Rockefeller Plaza, New York City, before her move to CBS. At left is a picture of her husband, Maury Povich.

George McGovern's presidential campaign, Nixon's trip to the Soviet Union, and later, the Watergate scandal. She was bold, ambitious, and tireless. "I burrowed my way through the crowd of reporters and popped up in front," she told a magazine reporter. But Connie was also noted for the natural warmth of her personality. "Being confrontational is alright," said Walter Cronkite, who anchored the "CBS Evening News" from 1962 to 1981, "but Connie Chung also always remained civil. She was able to ask tough questions in an intelligent way." In 1976, she became an anchor at a CBS affiliate in Los Angeles. By 1983 Connie was working the national news as weekend anchor for NBC.

During her climb to the top, Connie focused all her energy and time on her career, which meant many personal sacrifices. Her work demanded red-eye flights, rigid schedules, and many lonely Saturday nights. For Connie, fame and recognition also brought isolation and loneliness. It wasn't until she married Maury Povich, a daytime television talk show host, that she began to find happiness in her personal life.

Connie first met Maury in 1969 at WTTG-TV. At the time, Maury hosted "Panorama," a Washington, D.C., talk show. He was 30 and married. Connie and Maury became casual friends, and they kept in touch after Connie left for a new job in Los Angeles. By 1976, she was anchoring three daily newscasts while Maury, having been fired from several jobs as a result of his continuous disputes with network executives and producers, anchored a news show in Chicago. Another contract dispute resulted in his leaving Chicago, and he wound up at the CBS affiliate in Los Angeles where Connie was also working. Their friendship deepened, but the time was short—four months later, Maury was fired again. At the same time, his wife demanded a divorce. Under the strain, his self-confidence fizzled and he became depressed. He increasingly called on Connie for moral support and found her to be the most reliable friend he had.

Maury eventually took a job as a news anchor in San Francisco. He and Connie called each other regularly, soon realizing that their friendship was taking a different turn. They began to date. But Maury was fired yet again, and a new job took him even farther away from Los Angeles, to Philadelphia. They continued their relationship on a long-distance basis and ultimately their patience paid off. Maury returned to Washington to host "Panorama" again in 1980. Soon

Constance (Connie) Yu-Hwa Chung

In 1983, Connie Chung took over as hostess for NBC's "Today Show" after Jane Pauley, on the left, took maternity leave.

Connie joined CBS in New York. With the renewed proximity, they saw more of each other.

While neither Connie nor Maury made a formal proposal to marry, Connie remembers the moment the decision was made. She was in Bendel's, an exclusive clothing store in New York, shopping for a cocktail dress. Seeing nothing that interested her, she wandered into the bridal department, spied three dresses that caught her fancy, and tried them on. The second dress, made of antique satin and lace, fitted her perfectly. She saw it as a good omen. She ran to the phone to call Maury. "Now we can get married," she announced excitedly, "I found the dress." Maury's family reacted uncomfortably to the news that Maury's new bride was not Jewish, but Chinese American. But their initial reservations soon gave way to good wishes. As for the Chungs, Connie's parents were greatly relieved to learn that their daughter, at the age of 38, was finally getting married.

Connie and Maury did not actually live together until two years later, when he was hired to host "A Current Affair," a talk show based in New York. He and Connie moved into a spacious apartment overlooking Central Park. They also bought a country retreat in New Jersey.

In 1988, Connie returned to CBS with a weekend show called "Saturday Night with Connie Chung." This was followed, in 1990, by a popular weekday program called "Face to Face." At 43 years of age, Connie was happily married and astoundingly successful. But she chose that year, for the first time in her life, to make a professional sacrifice for the sake of a long deferred, deeply personal wish. She stunned the press and the public when she announced her reasons for leaving "Face to Face." "I now need to take a very aggressive approach," she declared, "to having a baby." Connie, having decided that candor was the best policy, was not at all prepared for the media's subsequent assault on her private life. Connie and Maury's efforts to conceive were sensationalized and made the butt of many late-night television jokes.

It was a painful time for the couple. Connie came to symbolize the doubt and ennui of a whole generation of American women who had delayed maternity to pursue their professional dreams. The embarrassment was compounded by the fact that her attempts to conceive with Maury were repeatedly unsuccessful.

With the announcement that, beginning June 1, 1993, Connie would coanchor the "CBS Evening News" with Dan Rather, as well as host her own news magazine show, "Eye to Eye with Connie Chung," Connie was thrust into the limelight anew. The news was celebrated in the Asian American community, but greeted with both skepticism and criticism in the media. In the opinions of Connie's harshest detractors, her strength as a television personality was her likeability, not her capacity to report and analyze the news, and her abilities as a journalist did not run deeper than reciting what appeared on the teleprompter. "Ms. Chung's most common expression is a blank earnestness," snapped Walter Goodman of the *New York Times.* Critics who accused her of superficiality had plenty of ammunition in view of the light celebrity and fluff pieces that had aired on her shows with titles like "Life in the Fat Lane" and "Stressed To Kill." Connie admits that these shows injured her reputation as a journalist. "That was a hurtful period," she recollected, "Those programs earned me a miserable reputation."

Coanchorpersons of the "CBS Evening News," Dan Rather and Connie Chung.

Other skeptics charged that Connie's selection to coanchor the nightly news had less to do with her merits as a journalist and more to do with ratings. Her astronomical Q-rating, an industry measure of a television celebrity's recognizability and popularity, would undoubtedly boost the sagging ratings of the "CBS Evening News," which had trailed behind ABC's "World News Tonight," anchored by Peter Jennings, since 1989. Indeed, the "Evening News"'s ratings jumped 6% the day after Connie's debut as coanchor.

Connie, as well as her defenders, pointed out that she paid her dues covering hard political news. Even if her subsequent programming had not given her an opportunity to grow as a journalist, with the "Evening News" and "Eye to Eye," she hopes to earn her reputation back. Her supporters predict that despite the criticisms, her accessibility, her warmth, her sincerity, and her vivacious sense of humor—not to mention her capacity for sheer hard work—will sustain her.

Some of the harshest criticism of Connie has come from inside the Asian American community. At the 1993 conference of the Asian American Journalists Association, she flew into San Francisco to deliver the keynote address. Some participants at the conference wondered aloud why Connie, not only the top Asian American in broadcast journalism but perhaps the most famous Asian American in the world, hadn't lent her support to the Asian American community earlier.

During the address, which was broadcast globally, she responded to this criticism in classic Chung style, with honesty, humor, and humility. "I have no good answer for not being involved. I have been terribly remiss," she said. "I've been flying blind, trying to survive, plugging away at my little career."

Connie offered to mentor midcareer members of the association and promised more involvement in promoting the aspirations of young Asian American journalists. Because Chung has reached the summit of her profession, she can share her success in tangible ways. In so doing, she has acknowledged her greatest, if unintended, legacy: putting an Asian face where millions of Americans had never seen one, breaking barriers for the dreams of the next generation.

U.S. senator Daniel Inouye.

Senator
Daniel
Inouye

DANIEL INOUYE WAS BORN IN HONOLULU, HAWAII, ON September 7, 1924, into a family which deeply valued dignity and honor. As he grew, he continued that legacy, and in the process he became a decorated military hero and a political leader of enormous influence.

Four generations before, in Yokoyama, his family's home village in Japan, Daniel's great-grandfather, Wasaburo Inouye, accidentally caused a fire that destroyed his own house as well as two others. Daniel's grandfather, Asakichi Inouye, wanted to pay for the loss. But he knew that as long as he remained in Japan, he would never earn enough money to do so. He left Yokoyama for Hawaii and took a job working in the sugarcane fields for $10 a month. With several years of savings, he repaid the debt and restored the family's honor.

Daniel grew up in a tiny house in a neighborhood considered to be the first Japanese slum in Hawaii. His family was poor but proud, and they believed strongly in family commitment and in hard work. Daniel's first hero was his father, Hyotaro Inouye, who worked two jobs to support the family and put all four of his children through college.

Daniel attended Honolulu public schools. He earned money by parking cars at the old Honolulu stadium and by giving haircuts to his classmates. As hobbies, he kept a flock of homing pigeons and a stamp collection, built crystal radios, and experimented with chemistry. But soon World War II would engulf his young life. On December 7, 1941, Japan attacked an American military installation at Pearl Harbor. Daniel, who had received medical aid training, was called to help manage the civilian casualties.

The impact of the attack on Japanese Americans was devastating. Japanese Americans had worked hard to become a part of American society. But the attack provoked an anti-Japanese hysteria that swept the country. Many Americans, especially those of European descent, viewed Japanese Americans as enemies and outsiders, even though many were born in the United States and saw themselves as Americans. "White men would sneer as we passed," Daniel recalled. "We felt it in school when we heard our friends and neighbors called 'Jap lovers.'"

Japanese Americans, especially the American-born Nisei, wanted to demonstrate their loyalty to the United States by joining the war effort, but they were barred from joining the armed forces. Those who were already in the army were transferred to noncombat units. Shortly after the attack on Pearl Harbor, President Franklin D. Roosevelt signed Executive Order 9066, which mandated the internment of all Americans of Japanese ancestry until the end of the war. Japanese Americans were evacuated from the West Coast and transported to internment camps around the country. Each internee was only allowed to bring to the camp what would fit into a single suitcase. They were forced to abandon everything else they owned, including their land and homes. As a result of the order, Japanese Americans lost an estimated $400 million in property. But what the order cost in emotional terms to the 112,000 people whose lives it devastated was immeasurable. And while the order was put forward as a security measure, it was clearly also motivated by racial prejudice—German and Italian Americans were not subjected to the same humiliation while American forces waged war with Germany and Italy.

In spite of the indignity of the order, scores of young Nisei pled for a chance to fight. Six months after the attack on Pearl Harbor, the War Department agreed to put soldiers of Japanese descent who were already on active duty into a special combat unit, the 100th Infantry Battalion, but it refused to accept new recruits. On January 22, 1943, however, the department created the 442nd Regimental Combat Team for Japanese American recruits. On that day, hundreds of Japanese Americans in Hawaii volunteered to join the regiment, and nineteen-year-old Daniel was among them. Even as thousands of Japanese Americans languished in internment camps, he said, "Americanism is not, and never was, a matter of race or ancestry."

In April 1943, Daniel and 2,600 other young Japanese American recruits arrived at Camp Shelby, Mississippi, for basic training. They were driven to excel, and in every exercise they outdid the other recruits. They were not only training for the war, but fighting for the honor of their

Senator Inouye, as chairman of a Senate subcommittee holding hearings on competitiveness in children's television programming, gets some cogent advice from Big Bird of Sesame Street.

families in the camps. They wanted once and for all to silence those who had suspected Japanese Americans of disloyalty. Nearly all the officers at the camp were white, and while most of the other soldiers accepted the Japanese American recruits, some still viewed them with hatred. This did not in the least discourage the Nisei. They attacked every combat exercise with a fury. Their motto became "Go for Broke."

During the training, a few hundred recruits were sent to Africa to reinforce the 100th Infantry Battalion, while the rest waited impatiently to join the action. A year later, they got their chance. Their destination was Italy. From June to September 1944, the 442nd Regimental Combat Team fought the German army valiantly. With victory after victory, they advanced 50 miles between the towns of Suvereto and Vecciano, driving Hitler's forces into the mountains.

Meanwhile, in northeastern France, General George Patton led the Allied advance to the German border. American forces were locked in furious combat with Hitler's forces in the steep, forest-covered Vosges mountains. The 442nd joined the Seventh Army there in the dead of winter to carry out a critical mission. The 1st Battalion, 141st Infantry, was trapped in the mountains, surrounded by advancing German forces, with their communications and supplies cut off. The 442nd Regimental Combat Team was ordered to rescue the unit before it was destroyed.

At 4 A.M. on October 27, 1944, they set out for the rescue. The German forces attacked the approaching team with machine guns, artillery, mortars, and hand grenades. By the end of the second day, American forces had advanced only 500 yards and suffered many casualties. The trapped battalion was running out of medical supplies, food, water, and ammunition. But by the end of the third day, with half their men dead or wounded, the 442nd was only 700 meters from the battalion. The following morning, they barraged the remaining distance with artillery, took the last German roadblock, and rescued the battalion. Because the battalion was made up of young men from Texas, they gratefully dubbed members of the 442nd "Honorary Texans."

With 1,800 of its soldiers hospitalized, the team was severely depleted. For the next six months, the regiment rested. But in March 1945, they returned to Italy. Germany held a defensive line, known as the Gothic Line, through the mountains from the east coast of Italy to the west coast. The 442nd was ordered to drive German forces from the mountains at the western end.

On the night of April 4, 1945, they scaled the 2,800-foot-high Mount Fragolita in total darkness. The following morning they eliminated the German encampment at the top of the mountain. By April 21, the team had vanquished the Germans on every mountain in their sector except one—Colle Musatello. It would be the site of Inouye's greatest heroism.

Inouye, who was then a second lieutenant, led a platoon up the ridge of Colle Musatello. First they circled and destroyed a German mortar observation post. When the platoon was 40 yards away from the main German defenses, they were attacked by three machine gun units. Inouye pulled the pin on a grenade and ran toward the nearest machine gun nest. A bullet ripped into his stomach, but that did not stop him. He threw the grenade into the bunker and killed the rest of the crew with his rifle. He threw two more grenades at the second machine gun nest. Ten yards away from the third machine gun nest, Inouye pulled the pin on his last grenade.

51

As a young man during World War II, Inouye volunteered for the all-Japanese American 442nd Regimental Combat Team, which fought in Italy and Germany and became the most decorated combat unit of the war. Inouye lost an arm in Italy while single-handedly destroying several German machine gun nests.

But at that moment a German soldier stood up and fired at him with a rifle grenade, all but blasting off his right arm. His last grenade was still clutched in the hand which dangled lifelessly next to him. With the hand that remained, he pried the grenade loose and threw it, destroying the third machine gun nest. He stumbled to his feet and continued to move toward the bunker, firing his rifle with his left hand, until a bullet hit him in the leg and felled him.

Forty-eight hours later, the Germans in the sector gave up. On May 8, Germany surrendered, and the war in Europe was over. The 442nd Regimental Combat Team returned to the United States as heroes. They were reunited with their families, who were newly released from the camps, ready to start their lives over again. President Harry Truman presented members of the team with their seventh Presidential Distinguished Unit Citation. "You fought not only the enemy," he said, "but you fought prejudice—and won." On July 26, 1948, the president outlawed segregation in the armed forces.

Inouye woke up in a hospital bed in Italy. The first thing he thought as he regained consciousness was that he would never be able to play the ukelele again. He spent 20 months recuperating in Naples, then in New Jersey and Michigan before he returned to Hawaii. He was awarded the Distinguished Service Cross, the Bronze Star, a Purple Heart, and a dozen other medals and citations. But his heroism did not immunize him from racism. In San Francisco, on his way back to Hawaii, a barber turned him out of his shop, telling him, "We don't cut Jap hair."

Inouye was too busy to become depressed about the loss of his arm. He originally planned to study to become a surgeon, but without his arm this plan became impossible.

The results of an aptitude test told him that his talents might be well-suited to public service. So he enrolled in the pre-law program at the University of Hawaii with dreams of pursuing a career in government.

While he was in college, he met Margaret Awamura. On their first date, he took her to a party at Fort Shafter with some of his friends from the army. On the second date, he took her out to dinner and proposed, and she said yes. When Inouye graduated, the two moved to Washington D.C., where he attended the George Washington University Law School and she worked for the Navy Department.

After Inouye completed his law degree, the couple returned to Hawaii, and he began to participate in the activities of the Democratic party. In the elections of 1954, while Hawaii was still a U.S. territory, Democrats won a majority of the seats in both the territorial House and Senate. Inouye was elected to a seat in the House, and he became majority leader. When Hawaii became a state in 1959, he ran for a seat in Congress and won his election by a landslide.

Within his first year in Congress, Inouye had a chance to sit on the House Foreign Affairs Committee. But because of the importance of agriculture to Hawaii's economy, he asked instead for a seat on the House Agriculture Committee. After his first term expired, Inouye ran to represent Hawaii in the U.S. Senate, and won. In July 1964, Margaret gave birth to their son, Daniel junior.

As a U.S. senator for nearly three decades, Inouye has earned a reputation for keeping a low profile, for avoiding partisan rivalry, and for exerting his influence, whenever possible, behind the scenes. On numerous occasions, however, Inouye has been entrusted with the delicate and conspicuous

In 1993, Wilma Mankiller, chief of the Cherokee Nation of Oklahoma, First Lady Hillary Rodham Clinton, and Senator Inouye, here serving as chairman of the Senate Committee on Indian Affairs, prepare to discuss health care.

role of leading investigations into government misconduct. In 1973, he was in the national spotlight as a member of the Senate committee that investigated the Watergate scandal. In the mid-1970s, he headed the Senate committee organized to monitor the U.S. Central Intelligence Agency. In 1984, as Chairman of the Select Committee on Secret Military Assistance to Iran and the Nicaraguan Opposition, he led the investigation into allegations that U.S. officials close to President Reagan had illegally sold arms to Iran to raise money for antigovernment rebels in Nicaragua.

None of these important responsibilities diminished his loyalty to his home state. He makes a point of personally responding to his constituents as much as possible; personal representatives on each of the islands keep the senator informed about Hawaiians' opinions and concerns, and he himself makes dozens of trips between Hawaii and Washington, D.C., each year. Senator Inouye's activity in the Senate has had a beneficial impact on the quality of education and health programs in the state. In addition, in 1981 he helped to pass legislation to protect Hawaii's most important agricultural industry—sugar—from competition from exports. Because of what he has done for the good of his state, Senator Inouye remains enormously popular among Hawaiian voters.

After nearly three and a half decades in Congress, Senator Inouye is perhaps the most powerful Asian American in the U.S. government. As chairman of the Select Committee on Indian Affairs, which has jurisdiction over federal programs affecting native Hawaiians, Inouye has campaigned for the establishment of health care and education programs for Hawaii's native population. He also wields enormous influence as chairman of the Senate Appropriations Subcommittee on Defense, which decides how much money the government spends on the military. He is also chairman of the Senate Commerce, Science, and Transportation Subcommittee on Communications.

Throughout his career, Senator Inouye has led the life of a classic storybook hero. He overcame the obstacles of poverty and racism to become a military hero and an influential political leader. Throughout, he has remained loyal to his family, to his fellow Hawaiians, and to his heritage. In 1968, he delivered the keynote address for the Democratic National Convention. In his speech, "This Is My Country," he pleaded for harmony, faith, and pride in the face of the conflicts that racked the nation—student protests, race riots, and the bloody military campaign in Vietnam. He closed his address by invoking the many meanings of the Hawaiian greeting, "Aloha."

"To some of you who have visited us, it may have meant 'hello,'" he said. "To others, Aloha may have meant 'good-bye.' But to those of us who have been privileged to live in Hawaii, Aloha means 'I love you.' So to all of you, my fellow Americans, 'Aloha.'"

Doctor David Ho.

Dr. David Ho

IN THE LATE 1980S, NEW YORK, WITH ITS HUGE POPU-
lation of people with HIV and AIDS, was the epicenter of
the AIDS epidemic in the United States. But despite the
disease's devastating impact on the city, New York lagged
behind other cities in the United States and Europe in the
creation of a major center for research on AIDS. In 1988, the
Aaron Diamond Foundation convened a group of concerned
people to discuss the establishment of a world-class AIDS
research institution in New York City. The project became a
partnership between the foundation, the New York City
Department of Health, and the New York University School
of Medicine. Each partner had something vital to contribute
to the venture. The Aaron Diamond Foundation agreed to
provide seed money of $11 million for the renovation and
start up of the center. The city government agreed to provide
an entire floor in one of its buildings for twenty years, free of
charge, as well as an additional $3.4 million for renovation,
the largest amount of money the city has ever allocated for
medical research since the search for a cure for polio in the
1940s. The NYU Medical School gave the center access to
its large AIDS and HIV-positive patient population, as well
as an academic base from which the center could recruit the
best scientific talent in the world.

In 1989, after an international search, a team of
scientists recruited Dr. David Ho, a young medical researcher
at the University of California at Los Angeles, to run the
center. Since the center's opening in 1991, Dr. Ho, its scientific director and chief executive officer, has figured promi-
nently in the global fight against AIDS.

He was born in 1952 in Taiwan. His father, an
electrical engineer and computer scientist, left mainland

China for Taiwan, like many of his compatriots, in the late 1940s. He came to the United States during the late 1950s to attend graduate school. The rest of the family—David, his mother, and two brothers—joined him in Los Angeles in 1965, when David was 12 years old. David's mother, who was native Taiwanese, worked for a while as a manager of a jewelry manufacturing firm. Both of his parents are retired now and live in southern California.

When David first arrived in the United States, he was years ahead of his classmates in math, but knew only a few words of English. He grew up and attended public school in the Clifford Park area of Los Angeles. In high school and college, he was an avid athlete who played tennis and point guard on his high school and college junior varsity basketball teams. He also played chess competitively, once placing first at a tournament among chess teams from colleges throughout California.

David's interests were in math and science. He began college at the California Institute of Technology studying physics, with the idea of eventually working on research problems in astrophysics and subatomic physics. But gradually he came to feel that these fields were too abstract for him. At that time, medical technology was rapidly changing, and with the growth of molecular biology and the emergence of new diagnostic tools, medical researchers were better equipped to address pressing health problems. These developments caught David's attention. While he was still attending Cal Tech, he decided to switch his major to pre-med, with the ambition of pursuing a career in medical research.

Dr. Ho consults with his colleagues at the Aaron Diamond AIDS Research Center in New York City.

David met his wife Susan, an aspiring artist who also hailed from Taiwan, through friends while he was an undergraduate. While David attended Harvard Medical School, she studied for a degree at the Boston Museum of Fine Arts. The couple now live with their three children, Catherine, 15, Jonathan, 12, and Jacqueline, 7, in Chappaqua, New York.

David learned about AIDS as he completed his clinical training in internal medicine at UCLA Medical School.

He was interested in exploring possible links between infections and other diseases that aren't normally associated with it, like arthritis. While he was chief resident at UCLA at the end of the 1970s, he was one of the first doctors in the country to encounter patients with Acquired immune deficiency syndrome (AIDS). At that time, a small number of patients, mostly young gay men, were entering the hospital and dying of an array of illnesses that would not normally have afflicted young, healthy people. The makeup of their symptoms implied a breakdown in the immune system, the system of physiological mechanisms that resist infection and illness. David and his colleagues realized that what they were seeing was a new disease.

The patients came into the hospital more and more frequently, and in greater numbers. By the time the disease was named AIDS, David had seen approximately 150 patients who were diagnosed with it. As he began to do research full-time, he decided to concentrate his efforts on the study of AIDS and on the factors that cause the immune system to break down. One of the first questions about the disease was, how was it spread? He thought that one possibility was a transmissible agent, like a virus, a bacteria, or a fungus. In 1983, the Louis Pasteur Institute in Paris identified the cause of AIDS as the human immunodeficiency virus, or HIV.

By the time Dr. Ho was recruited to run the Aaron Diamond Center, he had already made a name for himself as a pioneer in AIDS research, with an impressive list of contributions to the medical community's understanding of the disease. In 1984, he and his colleagues at Harvard were the first to isolate HIV in semen, and to identify the existence of a carrier state in which individuals can be HIV-positive without developing any symptoms. The following year, he proved that HIV levels in saliva were extremely low, and therefore the virus could not be transmitted through casual contact. Some of Dr. Ho's other research was central to the development of a technique of measuring HIV levels in blood. He examined how the virus spread in the nervous system and the brain, thus facilitating research in AIDS dementia. Early on in the crisis, he had warned that AZT, the antiviral drug most commonly used to treat AIDS, would have limited effectiveness due to the emergence of resistant strains of HIV.

When he first arrived at the facility provided for the Aaron Diamond AIDS Research Center, it was a bare space, equipped only with a phone. But in 1991, when the center

Doctor Ho's workload rarely leaves him much time for his family, but he doesn't regret his intense commitment to his job.

officially opened its doors, it boasted 20,000 square feet of spacious laboratories equipped with state-of-the-art equipment, plush office space, a conference room, and a library. Congenial and unassuming, Dr. Ho quickly established a casual, friendly working environment, in which a staff of 50 scientists work energetically and creatively on different research projects. Because the institute is so large, they can tackle a variety of projects at once.

One focus of the center's research is HIV pathogenesis, the study of how HIV causes the disease and how it kills certain cells in the immune system. Why does HIV cause illnesses that kill certain individuals in a year or two, while other individuals live with infection for fifteen years and remain healthy? In patients who quickly develop AIDS symptoms, HIV is found to replicate at an explosive rate. In patients who are healthy for over a decade, there are very low levels of the virus. Moreover, there are different strains of the virus, each having different strengths. Healthy individuals may have been infected with weaker, "attenuated" strains of the virus that don't grow as well as other strains. In addition, there is a range of human responses to infection; some individuals are able to mount a stronger resistance to HIV than others. By studying different populations of people with HIV and AIDS and the variety of human immune responses, researchers hope to find keys to how the virus functions. Researchers also study how the virus is transmitted from person to person, through sexual contact and through pregnancy, to devise strategies to prevent transmission. Another focus is the chemical and genetic structure of the virus and the different stages of its life cycle. A look at all of the facets

of the disease are necessary for the design of a vaccine to protect the uninfected, as well as the development of drugs that will attack and destroy the virus in those who are infected.

Doctor Ho in his
New York office.

Scientists at the center have made important contributions to current knowledge of the disease. For instance, the center established that AIDS is a virally driven disease (while some scientists continue to debate whether HIV causes AIDS, Dr. Ho feels that the causal relationship between HIV and AIDS is indisputable). The institute has also identified the cells that are targeted by HIV in the body: lymphocytes, or T-cells, which regulate the immune system, as well as monocytes, which are located in certain tissues in the liver and brain.

Dr. Ho's work is intense and all-consuming; weeks
and months pass before he has any free time for himself and
his family. He goes to Taiwan nearly every year to lecture. In
the summer of 1994, for the first time, the entire family will
go together. To relax, he plays tennis with colleagues, and the
family usually escapes to Colorado for a week every year to
ski.

But Dr. Ho doesn't regret the workload. He believes
that in the long run, history clarifies the meaning of people's
contributions, however insignificant they appear at the time.
At this time, individual medical discoveries about HIV are
overshadowed by the staggering dimensions of the epidemic,
which, after a decade and a half, has taken hundreds of
thousands of lives. There are over twenty million people with
AIDS worldwide, and the number is expected to grow to fifty
million by the end of the century.

Still, Dr. Ho is encouraged by the breakneck pace at
which the scientific community has increased its understanding of the disease. Doctors first saw patients with AIDS
in 1980 and coined a name for the disease in 1981. Between
1981 and 1983, researchers identified its causative agent. By
1984, a test was created to diagnose the infection. From 1984
onward, the medical community has learned more about HIV
than it has learned about any other virus, including the viruses
that cause influenza and herpes.

Dr. Ho remains cautiously optimistic about the pros-
pects of finding a vaccine and a cure. The disease continues
to mystify experts, and a mass of research problems remain to
be solved before any solutions appear on the horizon. Today
there are only a few drugs available to treat the disease. In the
near future, however, Dr. Ho foresees significant advances in

the development of drug therapy. With the improvement and increase in the number of drug therapies—and a knowledge of how they can most effectively be combined—doctors can control the progress of the disease and prolong the lives of patients for years.

"You can have a tremendous amount of knowledge gain without a direct practical application coming out," Dr. Ho explains, "But you need all of this. Eventually you reach a certain threshold, and then you have a meaningful application. When that will come along, we don't know. It's like trying to build a large structure. There's no other way but to lay it piece by piece."

Fashion designer Josefina (Josie) Cruz Natori.

Josefina Cruz Natori

ON SEVENTH AVENUE IN NEW YORK CITY, THE CAPITAL of America's garment industry, categories are strictly enforced from the design class to the showroom—"day" versus "evening," "inner" versus "outer," and "sports" versus "formal." On the American fashion scene, distinguished among the world's fashion capitals for the practicality and comfort of its clothes (as well as for its conservatism), Josie Natori arrived with a concept for women's clothing that originated in her firsthand understanding of the needs of modern professional women, of their attitudes about who they are and what they want to wear. "Women have spent so much time in the last 15 years trying to go up the corporate ladder, trying to conform," she said. Natori's clothing, which is simple, sexy, and elegant, is designed to be worn by women for their own pleasure. It was a concept that revolutionized the industry.

Just as Madonna popularized wearing corsets, bustiers, and lace bras onstage and off, Natori was the first clothing designer to build a prestigious global multimillion dollar women's fashion house out of the anonymous and convention-laden lingerie industry. "We came in through the back door because the product made the name," she said. "We didn't start with the name and go through the ready-to-wear market, which is the normal way to launch a line." Adapting fabrics and silhouettes normally meant to be worn underneath other clothing or at home in bed—bras, bustiers, robes, and bodysuits in silk, satin, or velvet, embellished with lace or embroidery—Natori banished the frilly, the cute, and the boring from her line. She produced simple, luxurious garments that both recalled traditional Asian styles and shattered Seventh Avenue convention, capturing the imagination—and the purses—of fashion consumers worldwide.

A musical child prodigy, Josie Cruz was nine years old when she played her first piano solo with the Manila Philharmonic. Success was something she was raised to expect. "Filipino women are encouraged to be entrepreneurial," she said. "It's a very matriarchal culture. My grandmother always told me that women should be independent and have their own careers and never depend on a man for anything." She also believes that her experience with two cultures, in particular the sensitivity of Asian culture and the assertiveness of American culture, has served her well.

Josie moved to New York from her native Philippines in 1964 when she was seventeen, with ambitions of a successful career on Wall Street. Soon after graduating from Manhattanville College in 1968 with a degree in economics, she was hired by Bache Securities, a financial services firm, to set up a branch office in the Philippines. After three years, she joined Merrill Lynch in public finance, specializing in public utilities.

Josie met her husband, Ken Natori, a third-generation Japanese American, on a blind date. Petite, animated, and enthusiastic, Josie's personality complemented Ken's soft-spokenness. They married a year and a half later.

At the age of 30, by most standards, Natori had reached the pinnacle of success. She was the first woman vice-president in Merrill Lynch's investment banking division, and she earned an annual salary of $100,000. But after nine years, her work in finance felt routine to her. Eager to find new challenges, she and her husband Ken began to explore ideas for a business they could run together. They researched business ideas ranging from a car wash chain to a brokerage firm. "I started absolutely cold," she said, "I knew zilch about

the lingerie industry." What Natori did know was that she wanted to start a business that could combine her Filipino heritage with her experience as a woman.

After her son, Kenneth junior, was born, Natori quit her job in May 1977 and returned to Manila. Her first entrepreneurial venture—marketing baskets crafted in the Philippines—failed. But the embroidery and appliqué work on traditional Filipino clothing, largely ignored by the modern Filipino apparel industry, sparked her imagination. When she returned to New York, she brought a bag of embroidered cotton shirts around to different retailers. Initial response to her shirts was lukewarm. But a buyer at Bloomingdale's suggested that she make the blouses longer, turning them into nightshirts. "What's a nightshirt?" she asked. Nevertheless, she followed the suggestion, and the Natori Company was born.

The business started out slowly. Josie showed samples in their apartment and communicated with manufacturers in the Philippines by phone while Ken served drinks to potential

Josie Cruz Natori was a musical child prodigy, and performed with the Manila Philharmonic Orchestra when she was nine years old.

buyers and Kenneth junior watched from his crib. Within three months, she had sold $150,000 worth of orders for nightshirts.

In 1978, the Natoris took their first risk and invested $200,000 of their personal savings to lease a small showroom on East 34th Street in Manhattan. In 1980, her father, a contractor in the Philippines, built a half-million-dollar 60,000-square-foot factory for her company near Manila, where Natori's trademark embroidery and appliqué would be produced.

Because she lacked experience in the apparel industry, Josie continued to listen to retailers for design ideas. But eventually she began to add her own ideas: bold colors rather than traditional white and pink, and rich fabrics. By 1985, sales had grown to $10 million. Josie found that she could not handle the business alone, so Ken left his job as a managing partner at Shearson Lehman Hutton to help her. He became chairman and chief financial officer of the Natori Company.

What gave Josie and Ken an advantage over other fashion entrepreneurs was the business acumen they developed after years in the world of high finance. Their knowledge of economics, cash flow, risk assessment, and financial planning was critical to the company's growth from a small upstart to a high profile, global business. Another strength was Josie's personality. Warm and vivacious, always elegantly and simply dressed, Josie made a connection with her customers whenever she appeared in a store, and she listened to their ideas.

In 1987, *Working Woman* magazine gave Josie the Harriet Alger Award for her entrepreneurial achievements. That year, she also began to market her clothing in Europe by opening a retail and wholesale operation in Paris. The following year, the Philippine government honored her company for its promotion of Filipino exports.

In April 1991, Natori presented her first fashion show at the French Consulate in New York, attended by top retail executives and the editors of the major fashion magazines. Her collection was elegant and luxurious, showcasing the signature lingerie elements that have become her trademark: embroidered stretch-velvet leggings, beaded bustiers, satin gowns, and floor-length, appliquéd velvet wraps. When the show ended, it was clear that Natori had shaken the fashion establishment out of its slumber. She came out on the catwalk to take the bow that all designers take at the end of

A chicly dressed Natori poses next to some of her intimate creations.

a show, a moment of recognition and praise for the intense, around-the-clock work that goes into conceiving and showing a collection. But Josie was greeted with a thunderous standing ovation that moved her to tears. The ex-investment banker who had spent years trying to sell her ideas to the fashion world finally got her due.

Josie and Ken work side by side in their midtown Manhattan office. They have an ideal partnership—Ken watches the finances and tracks orders while Josie works on the creative side, developing new ideas and working with designers to realize them. But they are so rarely in the office at the same time that a meal together is a celebration. The busy Natoris live in an apartment on Manhattan's Upper East Side. They spend weekends at a country home in Pound Ridge in New York's Westchester County. Josie travels so frequently to Asia and Europe to oversee business that the couple has established a third home in Paris.

The company has grown so fast that Natori's vision of the company's role and interests has expanded beyond projections of sales and revenue. In April 1993, Natori put her stamp on the arts when she sponsored an exhibit at the Costume Institute at the Metropolitan Museum of Art. Richard Martin, curator of the institute, approached her with the idea of presenting a collection of clothes to show the history of innerwear's influence on outerwear, partially as a reflection of a larger debate in Western culture—the evolution of popular attitudes toward sexuality, and the blurring of the borders between private and public and between masculine and feminine. "People are shocked by the idea that lingerie is seen," Martin said, "but it has a 200-year history."

At the exhibit, 80 mannequins were dressed in clothing by design luminaries like Valentino and Balenciaga, as well as anonymous mass-market and custom-made European and American designs from the nineteenth and twentieth centuries. Also featured in the show was the gold corset by Jean Paul Gaultier that Madonna wore on her Blonde Ambition tour, as well as four of Natori's own designs. The show, which ran until the end of the summer, was seen by an estimated 250,000 visitors.

For Josie, as for many Filipino Americans, "home" is the Philippines. Deeply concerned for the well-being of her compatriots, when Mount Pinatubo exploded and left thousands of Filipinos without homes or livelihoods, she helped sponsor a concert to raise money for the relief efforts. "I want to be able to give something back, to do something for other people," she said. Some day she would like to open a foundation for children.

Her desire to make a difference in people's lives has also led to her involvement in public service. She volunteers for numerous organizations, including the Board of Trustees of Manhattanville College, the Philippine American Foundation, Junior Achievement, Inc., the International Women's Forum, and the Committee of 200. Josie has also lent her voice to the movement to make the American economy more hospitable for small businesses. Natori feels that American business culture has moved from a large, corporate orientation to a new interest in entrepreneurship, and that fostering the growth of small businesses will create jobs and spur the American economy. She participated in President Clinton's preinaugural economic summit in Little Rock, Arkansas. In

A successful investment banker before she became interested in designing lingerie, Natori felt that she needed a new challenge and went into business with her husband, Ken.

addition, she wrote a long letter to the president suggesting that he stimulate the economy by making credit more available to small businesses. "This means broadening guidelines or providing assurances to banks," she wrote, "in order to induce them to make loans." She also urged him to implement an investment tax credit and to take concrete action to address the growing health-care crisis.

The Natoris always have their eyes on expansion. Opening boutiques in large department store chains has assured wide distribution for the company. Natori specialty shops are currently housed in Bergdorf Goodman, Bloomingdale's, Saks Fifth Avenue, and I. Magnin. The company's clothing lines now include a "bridge" line, Natori II, of midpriced clothes that make Natori accessible to a wider range of customers. The Josie line, a less expensive line of lingerie, debuted in March 1993. With Donna Karan, Christian Dior, Fernando Sanchez, and Victoria's Secret on the lingerie market, the Josie line faces difficult competition. But the line has been performing so well that its first year revenue projection of $5 million has been changed to $8 million.

Licensing agreements have allowed Natori to share the risks and the costs of expansion with other companies.

Under such arrangements, Natori designs products that will be sold under the Natori name. A licensed manufacturer produces and markets the products and splits the profits with Natori.

In 1989, Natori signed a licensing agreement to produce towels and sheets. In spring 1993, the company reached out to the Asian market, starting with Japan, where Natori opened a dozen stores and signed a licensing agreement with Pola Cosmetics. She also opened a Josie boutique in Madrid and began to test a catalog in Spain, where a licensee also manufactures Natori slippers. Natori costume jewelry will be produced by a licensee in Canada. A line of fragrances is also sold. Ideas for swimwear, exercise wear, hosiery, footwear, handbags, scarves, home fabrics, rugs, wallpaper, and tableware are being developed for licensing.

In 1992, the Natori Company netted $30 million. It employs more then 1,000 people worldwide, and Natori's clothes and products are sold in 40 countries. By 1996, Natori expects the business to earn close to $200 million.

The first fifteen years of business were filled with hard lessons and mistakes. But Josie believed in her vision, and her patience and willingness to take risks have paid off. She feels that taking risks is an important aspect of any personal vision of success. "I never stopped taking risks, and you know you are going to make mistakes," she said, "and the trick or the challenge is to know when you make mistakes and to cut it short." In the future, Josie envisions furnishing an entire lifestyle—garments, accessories, linens, furnishings, bed and bath products—under the Natori name. For Natori, the sky is the limit.

U.S. representative Norman Mineta.

Norman
Mineta

KAY KUNISAKU MINETA, REPRESENTATIVE NORMAN Mineta's father, left Japan in 1902 and crossed the Pacific in a steamship bound for America when he was fourteen years old. He had intended to return to Japan after studying new farming techniques. But eventually he decided to stay, having saved enough money in ten years to send for his bride, the sister of one of his friends from back home. By the early 1940s, Kay Mineta was running a prosperous insurance agency in San Jose and raising two daughters and three sons in a comfortable home. His son Norman, who in 1974 would become the U.S. representative for the congressional district which included San Jose, was born on November 12, 1931.

U.S. laws prevented the Minetas and other immigrants from Asia from owning property in the United States. A local attorney agreed to hold property for Japanese American families until their oldest American-born child turned 21, at which age the property could be transferred back to the child. The attorney performed this favor for many Japanese American families in San Jose, and the Minetas were among them.

Norman had just celebrated his tenth birthday when Japanese forces attacked the U.S. military installation at Pearl Harbor. News of the attack touched off a fierce wave of anti-Japanese hysteria throughout the country. Japanese Americans, even if they had lived their entire lives in the United States, were viewed as enemy aliens and as a threat to national security. Within the Japanese American community, there was nervousness and fear. One day, police arrived without warning at the home of the Minetas' next-door neighbor, the director of a Japanese American social group, and summarily arrested him.

On February 19, 1942, President Franklin D. Roosevelt signed Executive Order 9066, a proclamation that ordered all American citizens of Japanese descent to be evacuated from the West Coast and held for the duration of the war in internment camps. In San Jose as in other communities, the order was posted on telephone poles and on the sides of buildings. For Japanese Americans throughout the country, it was a stunning humiliation. Their loyalty had been questioned. The order sent an unmistakable message that American society as a whole did not accept them.

Under new security laws, Japanese Americans were to remain indoors from 7 P.M. to 7 A.M. They were not allowed to travel in groups of more than five people, and they were barred from traveling more than 25 miles from their home without a special permit. Eventually, Kay Mineta's business was shut down and his broker's license was suspended. The family's savings accounts were confiscated, the contents of which the Minetas never saw again.

Finally, Japanese Americans were evacuated from the West Coast en masse. The evacuees were instructed not to bring more than they could carry. Some families were given only a few days' notice before they had to leave behind everything they possessed. Non-Japanese neighbors went from house to house, offering to buy the possessions of Japanese American families for a pittance. Young Norman was forced to give away his beloved dog, Skippy, and to leave behind most of his toys and belongings.

On May 29, 1942, the Minetas gathered with other families at the train station. Norman was dressed in his Cub Scout uniform. He brought his baseball bat and his catcher's mitt, but he decided to leave the bat behind, expecting it

would be confiscated as a dangerous weapon. On the train, drawn shades prevented the riders from seeing where they were being taken. Guards stationed at the ends of each car made sure no one tried to speak. When they reached the end of their ride, they were 400 miles from home.

The army had turned the Santa Anita racetrack into a makeshift camp. Each internee was given a mattress bag and instructed to stuff it with hay. Some internees were housed in barracks, but less fortunate ones were housed in the stables. The Minetas, a family of seven, occupied a tiny, 15-by-20-foot space that was packed with their beds. The showers were a dozen blocks away. As they tried to sleep, searchlights perched on nearby guard towers shone in their faces throughout the night. Three months later, the Minetas were moved again, this time to a camp that had been set up for more permanent occupancy at Heart Mountain, Wyoming. The internees, who had packed for California weather, were little prepared for the arid climate, the harsh sandstorms of summer, and the bitter cold of winter.

Norman Mineta—the young man on the left in the plaid shirt—with his family and friends at the Heart Mountain, Wyoming, internment camp where he was incarcerated during World War II.

There were 12,000 people in the camp. The Minetas occupied an 18-by-25-foot space equipped with a stove. They ate with the other residents in a large mess hall. Norman attended sixth grade at the camp school, and after school he played with friends. He also belonged to the camp's Boy Scout troop. The residents, knowing they would be kept in the camp until the war ended, did their best to make it home. But everywhere they looked, barbed wire, watchtowers, and armed guards reminded them that home was no longer what it should be.

In 1943, the Minetas were finally released from the camp, one by one. Kay Mineta was released first. He traveled to Chicago to take a job teaching Japanese to U.S. Army soldiers. In November, Norman and his mother were released. They boarded a bus outside the camp and stayed overnight in Butte, Montana, before catching a train that would reunite them with Kay. After Norman and his mother finished a meal at a restaurant, Norman stood to clear the table as he had

On the left, Senator
Daniel Inouye and
Representative Mineta look
on while President Jimmy
Carter signs a bill creating
a commission to look
into the wartime internment
of Japanese Americans.

always done in the camp. His mother gently reminded him that they were no longer in the camp, and he no longer had to bus his dishes.

After the war, droves of Japanese Americans left the camps and returned to their home towns to quietly reconstruct their lives. Most remained silent about the shame of the internment and tried in earnest to leave the painful memories behind. But younger generations of Japanese Americans, born in the United States, could not forget the pain of having their sense of identity and their loyalty questioned. For Norman, vivid memories of the internment and the unjust way in which the government had treated Japanese Americans during the war fueled his desire to make a career in public office.

Norman graduated from San Jose High School and went on to study business at the University of California at Berkeley, where he graduated in 1953. After graduation, Mineta joined the U.S. Army and served as a military intelligence officer in Japan and Korea. He left active duty in 1956, but he continued to serve in the reserves and eventually was promoted to the rank of major. When he left the reserves, he returned to San Jose to work for his father's reestablished insurance firm.

In 1962, Mineta secured his first public office as a member of the Human Relations Commission of San Jose. The city council then appointed him to serve with the San Jose Housing Authority. In 1967, Mineta was appointed to fill a vacated seat on the San Jose City Council, becoming the first person of color ever to sit on the council.

In 1971, he was elected mayor of San Jose, the first Japanese American to be elected mayor of a major U.S. city. Besides fulfilling his duties as mayor, he spoke aggressively on

*Congressmen Mineta of
California and Paul Simon
of Illinois confer during
a meeting of the House
Budget and Rules committees.*

the special concerns of all American cities, participating actively in the U.S. Conference of Mayors and the National League of Cities.

Three years later, the Republican congressman who represented California's 15th congressional district retired. The district, which includes major portions of Santa Clara and Santa Cruz counties as well as part of the city of San Jose, is the third most populous district in the state. Mineta saw in the vacancy an opportunity to finally participate in national policy-making. He ran for the seat and won it.

In his two decades in Congress, Representative Mineta has won admiration among his colleagues in the House of Representatives. Observing his tireless energy, his attention to detail, and the depth of his knowledge and understanding of public-policy issues, they have entrusted him with positions of authority in the House. Mineta has sat on numerous committees and subcommittees, allowing him to contribute to legislative action on a broad range of issues, including transportation, trade, industry, the space program, and the federal budget. As a member of the House Committee on Public Works and Transportation, he chaired subcommittees on surface transportation, aviation, and public buildings and grounds. In 1993, his colleagues elected Mineta chair of the committee. He was the first Asian American to chair a major committee in the House. President Clinton offered Mineta the post of U.S. Transportation Secretary, but he turned it down. He explained that he enjoyed working on a number of public-policy issues at once, and as secretary of transportation the focus of his work would be narrower.

But the political issue that brought him into the national spotlight was civil rights. Throughout his career, he has been vigilant and outspoken about the concerns of Asian Americans. In 1988, Mineta led other Japanese American legislators, including his fellow Californian Robert Matsui, in their campaign to pass H. R. 442, the Civil Liberties Act of 1988, which demanded redress for the indignities suffered by Japanese Americans during the war and a formal, national apology for the internment.

With a tremor in his voice, Congressman Mineta stood on the floor of Congress and recalled his painful memories. He painted a haunting image of the 10-year-old boy who was forced to leave his cheerful, comfortable childhood and everything familiar to him behind. He finished his speech to thunderous applause. Congress voted to pass the act by an overwhelming margin.

The victory was a small vindication for the 120,000 Japanese Americans whose lives had been uprooted, who lost everything they had, and whose sense of belonging was irreparably damaged. But it was an important triumph. Congressman Mineta had shared his memories with the nation and successfully ensured that the injustice and shame of the internment would never be forgotten.

Loida Nicolas Lewis.

IN 1987, AN AFRICAN AMERICAN LAWYER AND FINANCIER named Reginald Lewis stunned the business world by buying Beatrice International, a gigantic food conglomerate made up of 64 companies in 31 countries, for $985 million.

Before news of the purchase spread, Reginald Lewis had already made a name for himself as a maverick. From modest beginnings in West Baltimore—where he was raised by his mother, his stepfather, a postal worker, and his grand-parents—he eventually went on to Harvard Law School and began to work as a corporate attorney in New York. In 1970, he formed his own firm, which eventually became Lewis & Clarkson. After fifteen years of helping his clients to amass enormous profits, he decided to give corporate financing a try himself, forming his own investment firm, the TLC Group, in 1983.

The following year, he bought the ailing McCall's Pattern Company, a maker of sewing patterns, with $1 million of borrowed money, inheriting $24 million of corporate debt. His creative management of McCall's resulted in the com-pany's greatest profits in years. Just three years after buying McCall he sold it for $65 million, which left him with a huge profit, $90 for each dollar he had invested.

Lewis's subsequent purchase of Beatrice International firmly established him as a major player on Wall Street. In the African American community he was also celebrated as a hero and a role model, an African American success story in the classic Horatio Alger mold. Moreover, TLC Beatrice, already established as one of the largest food companies in the world, became the largest black-owned business in the United States.

Loida
Nicolas
Lewis

Reginald Lewis led a glamorous and fast-paced life. He counted among his friends celebrities and prominent politicians. He was a lover of good food and music, and his homes in New York, Long Island, and Paris were filled with valuable artwork. He also established a reputation for philanthropy, making generous donations to numerous organizations, including a $3 million grant to Harvard Law School, the largest donation ever made by an individual to the school, and $1 million to Howard University, a prominent black school.

Lewis's legend was brought to a devastating halt in 1993 when the company announced, on January 18, that he was being hospitalized for brain cancer and was in a coma. On the following day, he died. His responsibilities as chief executive were transferred to his half-brother, Jean Fugett, an attorney who had sat on the board of the company. But one year later, the company leadership changed again, in a way that took the business world completely by surprise. On February 1, 1994, Lewis's widow, Loida Nicolas Lewis, stepped out of her late husband's shadow and into the corporate limelight to assume the chairmanship of TLC Beatrice International. Beatrice remained America's largest black-owned company. But Loida Lewis, as chairperson, went from the symbolic role of corporate wife to a place among the most powerful Asian Americans in the corporate world.

The move was bold, but the life of Loida Lewis was filled with bold decisions and outstanding achievements, which had been all but eclipsed by her husband's phenomenal success. Throughout his career, despite his fame, Reginald Lewis had remained private about his personal life, and to the press he seldom spoke about Loida or about their daughters,

Leslie and Christina. In some speeches, he would refer to her as "the least materialistic person I know." The Filipino American community was familiar with Loida through her work as publisher of *Niñgas-Cogon*, a Filipino American magazine, and as one of the founders of the Asian American Legal Defense and Education Fund, a legal advocacy organization devoted to the special concerns of the Asian American community. But on Wall Street, little was known about her.

When Loida met Reginald, she was drawn to him because he reminded her of her father. Both men were dynamic, ambitious, creative—and completely self-made. Two years into prelaw studies at the University of the Philippines in Manila, Francisco de Jesus Nicolas was forced to abandon school because he could no longer afford the tuition. But his work as a lumber trader, cutting logs in his home province, Sorsogon, and selling the wood to a furniture company in Manila, proved lucrative enough for him to start his own company.

He met Loida's mother, Magdalena Mañalac, while she was in college majoring in pharmaceutical studies. When they were introduced, at a bowling alley, she took his hand and looked into his eyes. As Francisco later told his children, it was love at first sight.

In 1937, the lumber business became a furniture company, Nicolas Furniture, which was later renamed Nicfur and, to this day, continues to be one of the largest furniture companies in the Philippines. Francisco Nicolas's entrepreneurial exploits started with wood, but they did not end there. In the town of Sorsogon, the Nicolases also owned a drugstore, a gasoline station, a trucking and hauling company, not to mention the local bowling alley, a billiard hall, and a

Loida's husband, Reginald F. Lewis, who was chief executive officer of TLC Beatrice International Holdings, Inc., until his death in 1993.

87

Loida with the corporate executives of TLC Beatrice International.

chain of movie theaters, each of which was named after one of the three women in his life—his wife and his two daughters. The theater in town was named after the middle child, the older of the two Nicolas daughters. It was called the Loida Theater. While Loida was still a child, Francisco already believed that his daughter's outspokeness, her personality, and her grace would make her a great politician, and he joked that if she ever decided to run for office, she would have advance billing on the marquee of his theater.

Francisco's business ventures prospered and enabled the family to live comfortably in a large house in the center of the city. Francisco was a commuter who spent the week in Manila looking after the furniture company. The weekends were special occasions for the family, when Francisco returned to Sorsogon, bearing gifts and treats from Manila. The family would have sumptuous meals, and afterward sit on the veranda overlooking the city. Invariably Francisco would seize the opportunity to deliver his regular weekend sermon.

"Okay," he would begin, "What are the five secrets of success?" For Francisco it was vital that his children learn these "secrets," for he had already envisioned a future for each of them. Danny, the oldest, would succeed him as head of the family business. Jay, the second, would become an engineer. Loida, destined for a career in public service, would become a lawyer. Imelda, the younger daughter, or Mely, as she was called, would marry a banker. And Francis, the youngest son, would become an architect.

The secrets of success, as each child learned them, were hard work, common sense, perseverance, resourcefulness, and faith in God. The children were taught that nothing important is ever accomplished without time and hard work, or without exploring all the avenues for approaching a problem or opportunity. They were also taught that everything they did took place within a larger scheme, and that if for some reason they did not attain a particular goal, perhaps a different, even greater one was in store for them.

Loida excelled in school. She loved to read, and her favorite subjects were English and history. She also became a cheerleader for the volleyball team. When she graduated from high school, she was class valedictorian. She went on to St. Theresa's College in Manila, where she majored in humanities, studying English literature and general world history. Immediately after graduating with honors, she studied law at the University of the Philippines, where she graduated in the top 10% of her class in 1968.

To reward Loida for passing the bar exam, Francisco offered her the gift of a trip abroad. She decided to pay an extended visit to Mely, who was in New York studying for a master's degree at Columbia University. While Loida was in

New York, she landed a job as an administrative assistant at the Law Students Civil Rights Research Council. Her boss, Reynaldo Glover, quickly recognized that Loida was not at all an average secretary. Glover also happened to be dating Mely at the time, and for fun he invited Reginald Lewis, then a busy young attorney at a large corporate law firm in New York, to meet Loida for a double date. Reginald reluctantly agreed to join them. When he and Loida were introduced, Loida did what her mother had done with her father years ago: she clasped Reginald's hand warmly and looked directly into his eyes. The connection was instantaneous.

By the spring of 1969, Reginald and Loida had decided to get married. When it came time for Loida to return to the Philippines in June, she suddenly got cold feet and broke off the engagement. But on the flight back to Manila, she realized that she had made a mistake. Once she arrived, she telephoned Reginald and told him that she wanted to get married after all. Loida's family, realizing that she would be leaving for good, urged her to have him come to the Philippines and marry him at home with her family. Reginald soon followed Loida to the Philippines, and they were married in August 1969.

When the couple returned to New York, Loida took a job as a paralegal at Manhattan Legal Services, a legal advocacy firm for the underprivileged. Mely, back in the Philippines, had begun a newspaper that was critical of the dictatorship run by Philippine president Ferdinand Marcos and first lady Imelda Marcos. Since her full first name was also Imelda, Mely named the paper *Imelda's Monthly,* a play on words. Loida wanted to start an offshoot of the paper in the United States for the Filipino American community. With

*Loida and Reginald
pose with members
of Loida's family.*

financial backing from her husband, she began to publish
Niñgas-Cogon ("brushfire" in Tagalog), a monthly magazine
that she continued to publish until 1979. In 1973, she left
Manhattan Legal Services to give birth to their first daughter,
Leslie.

Because federal law required applicants for the bar
exam to be U.S. citizens, Loida could not obtain the necessary
qualifications to practice law in the United States. In 1974,
however, the Supreme Court struck down the citizenship
requirement. Loida immediately applied to take the bar exam
and passed it on her first try. She became, without attending
law school in the United States, the first Asian woman to pass
the New York bar.

Loida then applied for a job as an attorney for the
U.S. Office of Immigration and Naturalization Services
(INS). She was summarily rejected. With a superb academic
record, Loida could not make sense of the rejection. Suspect-

91

ing that her exclusion had something to do with her being Filipina, she filed a discrimination suit against the INS. The case took three years, but Loida's persistence paid off. In 1978, the administrative judge ordered the INS to submit the qualifications of the attorneys they had hired when they rejected Loida. The INS failed to produce the data, the judge awarded Loida the suit, including three years back pay, and the INS hired Loida as a general attorney.

Loida worked at the agency until 1990. When immigrants with alien status applied for citizenship, she evaluated their applications and approved those who were eligible. In 1986, she was promoted to work in the trial attorney section.

In 1988, one year after acquiring Beatrice, Reginald Lewis moved to Paris to manage the company's European operations. Loida took a leave of absence from the INS and moved to Paris with him, along with Leslie and Christina, their second daughter, who was born in 1981. Although the Lewises traveled frequently, they were based in Paris for the next three years. They rented and furnished a town house in the center of the city, behind the National Assembly.

In Paris, Loida was struck by the graciousness and the gentler pace of life that the French practiced. It reminded her of life in the Philippines, which contrasted sharply with the frenetic intensity of New York. While she was in Paris, she decided to use her knowledge of immigration law to write and publish three books designed to help immigrants through the often intimidating and bewildering process of becoming U.S. citizens. She also followed Reginald's work and was his informal adviser. While in Paris, she, like the rest of the family, learned to speak French. Loida loves Paris, and along with New York and the Philippines, she continues to call it home.

Loida Lewis has followed in her father's footsteps and assigned goals to each of her children. One of them, she decided, would become a lawyer, while the other would become a doctor. As if it were divinely planned, Leslie, now an undergraduate at Harvard, is in fact setting her sights on law school. And Christina, who is now in high school, has expressed a desire to become a doctor.

Since Reginald Lewis's death, all of Wall Street has waited with bated breath to see what will happen with the company, and much conjecture about Beatrice's future has circulated in the press. Faced, as her husband was several years earlier, with the task of leading Beatrice into the next phase, Loida is taking everything in stride, and she has avoided the relentless scrutiny of the press. She has chosen instead to let her actions speak for her. Since she became chairman, she moved quickly to cut costs, to sell assets to repay debt, and to open communications with shareholders. In July 1994, she assumed the additional post of chief executive officer of the company.

When she can, Loida escapes to her house at the ocean in East Hampton where, in the morning, she meditates and prays. With experience, courage, faith, with the love of her father and her husband, guided by the wisdom they passed on to her, nothing can faze her.

Chancellor Chang-Lin Tien and his wife Di-Hwa Tien.

Chang-Lin Tien

WHEN FIRST-YEAR STUDENTS ARRIVED TO REGISTER AT the University of California at Berkeley in September 1990, university chancellor Chang-Lin Tien, dressed down in a T-shirt, was there to welcome them in person. Anticipating the confusion, anxiety, and boredom that can arise during the first days of the semester, Tien had video monitors installed in the busiest administrative offices, and stand-up comedians and characters from *The Simpsons* cartoon show humored students while they waited to register. "I think we should do everything possible to make new and returning students feel comfortable," he said. "For many it will be their first time leaving home. I think if we come out to help them, it will lessen a lot of their anxiety and confusion."

But Tien's own debut as chancellor of the largest public university in the United States and as the first Asian American to lead a major American university was not so comfortable. He started his new job at a time when the university community was weathering the blows of a series of tragedies. In September 1990, a fire in a fraternity house killed three students. At the end of the month, a gunman held students hostage at a pub, eventually killing one student and seriously injuring seven others. Throughout each tragedy, Tien comforted victims and bolstered campus morale. With his warmth, responsiveness, understanding, and accessibility, he quickly earned the widespread admiration of faculty and students.

When Tien was chosen in 1990 from among 250 candidates to become the chancellor of Berkeley, some feared that his Asian heritage and his science background would make him a cold, technocratic leader, the last thing a university with 32,600 students and professors needs. But Tien's approach to leadership soon proved them wrong. As soon as he started, he began to stroll the sunny, sprawling campus daily, greeting faculty and students with a warm handshake and a smile and stopping to listen to their ideas and concerns. Before Tien arrived, many students had never even seen their chancellor. For most American college students, interaction with school officials amounts to little more than a handshake on the proscenium at graduation.

Berkeley, a world-class research institution that is also widely considered to be the best public university in the United States, earned a reputation as a hotbed of student protest and radical counterculture during the tumultuous 1960s. To this day, Berkeley's students have upheld the legacy of activism. There are over 330 registered student groups on campus, 100 of which are devoted to students of special ethnic backgrounds. "I feel that an active student body is very positive," Tien remarked. "This is in fact an important part of the academic and intellectual atmosphere. Everybody should feel free to search for the truth and have open discussions."

Some feel that Tien is tolerant and open-minded to a fault. For example, he waited months before suspending a student known on campus as Naked Guy, who attracted national media attention by attending class in the nude. Tien called a mentally disturbed man who broke into his house with a machete a "romantic revolutionary." So many strange incidents, demonstrations, and student protests have rocked the campus lately that the university has earned the nickname "Berserkley."

Although colleagues find Tien friendly and non-confrontational, he makes decisions based on what he feels is best for the university. Sometimes that means making decisions that are not necessarily popular. And he never makes promises he does not intend to keep.

He was born in Wuhan, China, in 1935 to a wealthy family that made its fortune in banking. But they were uprooted twice by war. When the Japanese invaded China at the beginning of World War II, the family fled to Shanghai. His father, Tien Yun-Chien, became the city's finance commissioner, and his income enabled the family to live comfortably in a large home with servants.

But one Sunday afternoon in 1949, Communist troops only 25 miles from Shanghai began to advance on the city. The family was forced to flee again, this time to Taiwan. Tien's greatest regret was losing his stamp collection. "I had many good stamps," he said, "and I lost them all."

Tien's family arrived in Taiwan as refugees, poor and bereft of the comforts they knew on the mainland. The following year, his father secured an important position as secretariat chief for the Nationalist government, and the Tien family was finally able to live as comfortably as they had before. But two years later, Tien's father died of a heart attack, and the family experienced hardship again.

At National Taiwan University, Tien studied for a degree in mechanical engineering. But the activity he enjoyed the most was basketball. He spent six hours a day on the basketball court and played on the university's varsity basketball team. For a brief spell, he even played as a semiprofessional in Taiwan.

Eventually, all but one of the children emigrated to the United States. In 1956, at the age of 21, it was Tien's turn. Once in the United States, he earned a master's degree

Chang-Lin Tien during his college years in Taiwan in the early 1950s.

in mechanical engineering from the University of Kentucky at Louisville. He went on to receive a second masters and a doctorate from Princeton in 1959, after which he joined the faculty at Berkeley. He became a full professor of mechanical engineering in 1968 and chaired the department from 1974 to 1981.

Tien served as vice-chancellor for research at Berkeley from 1983 to 1985. He then spent two years at the University of California at Irvine as executive vice-chancellor. There he led the move to recruit minority faculty, to institute multicultural and international course requirements for first-year undergraduates, and to invite the participation of the faculty in the administration of the campus. He earned a reputation for opening communication between faculty and administrators. He dispensed with formality, listened to teachers, and responded quickly and concretely to their ideas and concerns.

Along with his achievements as an administrator, Tien has achieved eminence as a scientist. He has written more than 200 scientific papers and is an authority on thermal radiation and heat transfer. When insulation tiles began to fall off the space shuttle in 1978, NASA called on Tien to help them correct the problem. The next year, he was again consulted for his expertise, this time in response to the threat of a disastrous meltdown at the Three Mile Island nuclear power plant in Pennsylvania.

Tien has received many honors, including a Guggenheim Fellowship and the Max Jacob Memorial Award, the highest honor in the field of heat-transfer physics. In 1962, at the age of 27, Tien became the youngest professor to win Berkeley's Distinguished Teaching Award. As an adviser, he has guided more than 60 graduate students to doctoral degrees.

When he first arrived in the United States before the civil rights era, his first impression of the country was of its racial intolerance. When he first got off the bus in Louisville, Kentucky, he saw the water fountains marked by signs that said "Whites Only" and "Colored." Tien was bewildered and didn't know which fountain to choose. It would not be his last experience with racism. One professor for whom Tien worked called him "Chinaman." Tien was not aware that the term was insulting until the other students told him. Even though he was afraid of jeopardizing the financial support that the school provided him, he confronted the professor and demanded to be called by his name. "The professor came right back and said, 'How can I remember all those strange names, Ching, Chong, Tong, Cong?'" Tien recalls. "I got so mad, I said, 'If you can't call me by my name, don't call me.'" For the next nine months, the professor didn't call Tien by any name. "But he never called me 'Chinaman' again," Tien says.

Tien had to survive with scarce financial resources. In Louisville, instead of eating at the school cafeteria, he walked to a poor section of town where he could find cheaper meals. When he moved to Princeton to earn his doctorate, he traveled two miles with his laundry to a dormitory where a load cost 40 cents less to wash than in town.

When he moved to California to teach at Berkeley, his family again encountered racism in their search for an apartment. The listings for some apartments on the north side of town were marked "Not for Orientals or Negroes." Even today, Tien's success does not immunize him from racism.

Chancellor Tien meets frequently with faculty and students and tries to keep abreast of their day-to-day problems.

Once when he went to cheer Berkeley's football team, which was playing a postseason game in Orlando, some of the opposing team's fans, using Tien's race to jeer Berkeley's team, chanted "Buy American! Buy American!"

Tien, whom colleagues claim has never lost his temper, has not allowed his experiences with hardship and racism to demoralize him. "I fear if I cannot channel those very unpleasant discriminatory experiences into a positive energy, into a constructive direction," he said, "then I'm not really doing the right thing for my own group or for the larger community."

Tien feels that his experiences as well as his cultural background give him a special perspective that serves him well as a university chancellor. On the one hand, he is realistic about the tensions that exist between different races. On the other hand, having seen the achievements of the civil rights era, the abolition of segregation and the integration of different groups in American society, he is optimistic about the possibility for change.

Tien is determined to do what he can to eliminate prejudice and racism at Berkeley. He supports Berkeley's "fighting words" policy, which disciplines students who verbally harass or abuse other students. "Fighting words" policies were established at Berkeley and other American campuses to combat hateful comments made to students about their sex, race, religion, or sexual orientation in an effort to create a respectful and tolerant environment in which students can focus on learning. "We have to maintain a certain level of civility on campus," he says. To combat prejudice and foster understanding on campus, Tien has also encouraged formal discussion groups on racial sensitivity.

Berkeley has seen profound changes in the racial makeup of its student body. When Tien arrived at Berkeley, the student body was 90% white. At the beginning of the 1980s, two-thirds of the undergraduates were white. The diversification efforts started by Tien's predecessor, Ira Michael Heyman, chancellor from 1980 to 1990, brought the arrival of more students of color. Since 1988 there has been no racial majority on campus. Today, only 39% of 22,000 undergraduates are white. Asians represent 31%, Latinos 15%, African Americans 7%, and Native Americans 1%.

Tien hopes to continue the diversification process by selecting 45% of each entering class on the basis of "diversity" rather than academic merit. He points out that if academic achievement were the only criterion for admission, Asian and white students would make up 94% of the student body. Opponents of affirmative action feel that enrolling more African American and Latino students rather than qualified Asian and white students will lead to a decline in academic standards and in student performance. Some Asian candidates who were denied admission to Berkeley charged that Berkeley used racial quotas against them. The controversy opened a Department of Education investigation of Berkeley's admissions process. Despite the criticism and controversy over the admissions policy, Tien points out that average grades and scores for all first-year students are at an all-time high, while dropout rates have fallen.

Tien feels that another great challenge facing the university will be the maintenance of faculty and academic excellence. By the turn of the twenty-first century many professors will retire. At the same time, over the next ten to fifteen years there will be a shortage of Ph.D.s in all fields, including the physical sciences, the social sciences, and the humanities. But unless academia takes on the task of training more professors, American universities in the twenty-first century will be faced with a scarcity of candidates for the openings that will become available.

Tien believes that this challenge offers a great opportunity for Berkeley and other American universities to diversify the makeup of their faculty, training and hiring more minorities for teaching positions. At Berkeley, 90% of the faculty is currently white, and 84% are male. While Asians comprise 26% of the entering undergraduate class, and Asians earn 15% of the Ph.D.'s, they account for only 5.6% of the faculty at Berkeley. Diversity in the student body at the

graduate school, the training ground for future professors, is also dragging, resembling the undergraduate school's makeup a decade earlier. To correct the lack of diversity among the faculty, Tien has instituted economic incentives, mentoring, and other programs to train, recruit, promote, and retain minority professors. As a result, 25% of new faculty hired are minorities and 26% are women.

President David Gardner insisted that Berkeley's selection of Tien to become its chancellor was based solely on his academic record and his solid reputation as a teacher and administrator. Nonetheless, Asian Americans celebrated Tien's appointment as an acknowledgment of the contribu-

Chang-Lin Tien laughs as he answers reporters' questions after University of California president David Garner, right, appointed him chancellor of the Berkeley campus.

tions Chinese and all Asian Americans have made to American society. To commemorate Tien's appointment, the Tang Foundation of San Francisco awarded Berkeley a $1 million grant, followed in 1992 by a second gift of $4 million. The appointment was also heralded as a long-overdue recognition of the university's diversity, where Asians make up one-third of the student body, as well as the diversity of the entire state. People of color make up 41% of California's residents. By the year 2000, the state will have no racial majority.

The challenge of diversifying the student body seems simple compared to the problem of confronting the university's budget crisis. The state has cut its funding from 40% of the university's budget in 1980 to 28.5% in 1992. This is one reason why tuition has increased 85% from 1989 to 1992, a difficult change to accept in a state that has long enjoyed low college costs in comparison to the East Coast.

One of Tien's responses to the budget crisis was to freeze faculty salaries and offer professors incentives to retire early. Tien's Chinese heritage has also strengthened Berkeley's ties with Asia and the Pacific Rim, creating new possibilities for financial support as well as for academic, cultural, and technological exchange programs. For instance, Tien got 16 Japanese companies to agree to provide partial funding for a computer mechanics laboratory.

Berkeley has managed to survive the economic recession that developed at the end of the Reagan-Bush era, thanks largely to Tien's contacts and ties to Asia. Tien travels frequently to Asia to talk to alumni and to marshal support for the university from Asian governments and companies. Taiwan's Education Minister Mao Kuo-Wen, a former student of Tien, facilitated a government grant of $400,000 to help create an Institute of East European Studies. A gift from Korean Air endowed a chair in Korean Studies. Currently, Berkeley professors teach economics to young Vietnamese diplomats in Hanoi. Student-exchange programs with six Asian countries are being developed, as well as the Pacific Economic Conference, which will bring Asian academic and business leaders to Berkeley to discuss topics ranging from trade to technology.

These days, Tien feels his greatest personal challenge is balancing his commitments. He is very devoted to his family. He and his wife Di-Hwa have three grown children, who all have both Western and Asian names: Norman Chihnan (meaning the very best wood), a microelectronics engineer; Phyllis Chihping (peaceful), a doctor; and Christine Chihyih (happy, outgoing), a student at Harvard's Kennedy School of Government. All of them graduated from Berkeley.

Tien has also continued to do research and to teach. He sympathizes with the criticism that academia often values the prestige of research over teaching. Tien finds that teaching, especially undergraduates, helps him to clarify his ideas for research. His new responsibilities as Berkeley's chief administrator have not kept him from teaching, and his lectures are directed specifically to first-year undergraduates.

Despite the challenges he faces as the university enters the twenty-first century, Tien, proud of the changes he has seen so far, is optimistic about the future, and happy to be doing what he does. "I feel so positive about the state, about the future," he says. "I never dreamed I would be chancellor of one of the greatest universities in the United States."

U.S. representative Robert Matsui, testifying in
1986 about his internment during World War II.

IN THE FALL OF 1993, PRESIDENT BILL CLINTON FOUGHT and won one of the toughest battles of his political career. He and his supporters convinced enough members of Congress to vote in favor of the North American Free Trade Agreement (NAFTA), a treaty which called for the reduction of barriers to trade and investment between Canada, the United States, and Mexico, with the ultimate objective of boosting the economies of all three nations.

The agreement was controversial, and opposition was strong and often hostile. Opponents charged that it would jeopardize jobs in the United States by encouraging U.S. companies to move manufacturing jobs to Mexico, where workers are paid far less. But supporters of the agreement countered that it would ultimately create jobs in the United States by eliminating Mexican barriers to U.S. exports.

As the war over NAFTA raged in the media and on the floor of Congress, Representative Robert Matsui, who was chosen by Clinton to be NAFTA's point person in Congress, was making the rounds of national television programs to promote the treaty. He appeared on "Meet the Press," the "CBS Evening News," the "MacNeil/Lehrer News Hour," and on C-SPAN and CNN. At the same time his wife, Doris Okada Matsui, deputy director of public liaison at the White House, promoted the treaty and explained its details to business groups and to the public.

NAFTA's successful passage in Congress enhanced Bob Matsui's chances of becoming chair of the powerful House Ways and Means Committee, on which he has sat since 1980. NAFTA's success also confirmed Doris Matsui's own talents for public service, not just as an activist and a political spouse, but as a political professional in her own right. The

Robert
Matsui and
Doris Okada
Matsui

107

critical and highly visible roles both Matsuis played in the passage of NAFTA made them one of the most talked-about political couples in Washington. Theirs was a political partnership in the style of Bill and Hillary Clinton, and it signaled a new era in the way men and women would participate in politics.

Doris Okada Matsui was born on September 25, 1944 in Dinuba, California, a small rural community in central California about 30 miles from Fresno. Her mother's father emigrated from Japan in the 1890s, when American law barred Japanese nationals from owning property. When Doris's mother was born, she was automatically an American citizen, and the family put all of their property in her name. Doris feels that this may have contributed to her mother's authority, to her strength and sense of responsibility.

Doris Okada Matsui.

These qualities set a good example for Doris, who worked hard in school and did well. "I wanted to succeed professionally," she said, "and I realized that I wanted to incorporate a family life into this whole thing too." In 1962, she left for Berkeley to enroll at the University of California, where she met Bob, an ambitious young law student. He, like she, was moved by John F. Kennedy's call to serve the nation, which had fired the imagination of an entire generation of young Americans, including the young Bill Clinton and Hillary Rodham. "Ask not what your country can do for you," Kennedy had said, "but what you can do for your country."

Bob Matsui was born on September 17, 1941. In December, Japan attacked U.S. military installations at Pearl Harbor. Subsequently, anti-Japanese hysteria in the United States rose to a feverish pitch. President Roosevelt issued Executive Order 9066 in response to a perceived threat to U.S. national security, and all "Japanese nationals" in the United States and their American-born descendants were incarcerated in internment camps. In April, when Bob was just six months old, he and his family were sent to an internment camp at Tule Lake, California.

The Matsuis were released when Bob was four years old, and they returned to Sacramento to quietly reconstruct their lives. "My parents rarely talked about it," he said, "since it was an issue of shame that our loyalty was put into question." But the emotional scars would eventually fuel Bob's drive to become a part of the American political system. Decades later, he and Representative Norman Mineta of San Jose, California, gave emotional testimony before Congress about the devastating impact the internment had wrought on the lives of Japanese Americans. Their testimony moved representatives to vote overwhelmingly in favor of the passage of the Civil Liberties Act of 1988, which mandated a national apology for the internment of Japanese Americans and redress payments of $20,000 to each internee. Symbolically, the act vindicated Japanese Americans and ensured that the internment would not become a forgotten chapter in American history.

Until Bob was 14, he wanted to be an architect. But he changed his mind when he read the autobiography of Clarence Darrow. A famous defense attorney in many dramatic criminal trials, Darrow defended labor leaders, a high school teacher who had broken state law by teaching Darwin's theory of evolution, and an African American family that had fought against a mob trying to expel it from a white neighborhood in Detroit. Darrow's work on behalf of the politically disenfranchised moved young Bob to become a lawyer with a commitment to public service. "[Darrow] said the basis of law was to protect the underdog, and that appealed to me. . . Bob said, "the need to protect those in need, who are not a part of the system."

Bob went to school at Berkeley. During his senior year, he met Doris, then a freshman at Berkeley, at a party. They knew each other for a year before they started dating, and by that time, Bob was in law school. When Bob graduated from Hastings and Doris graduated from Berkeley, they were married.

The young couple returned to Bob's home town, Sacramento, to begin their life together. Bob turned his efforts to setting up his own law firm. Since they knew that at first Bob would earn very little money, Doris worked for the state of California, first as a computer programmer and then as a systems analyst, to support them both. Bob began to make professional connections and to get referrals from other attorneys. By the end of his first year as an independent lawyer, his firm turned a profit. After three years, the practice was large enough for Doris to leave her job.

Doris seized this opportunity to devote her time to community activism. She became a member of various organizations, including the Junior League and the Sacramento Symphony League. She also became president of the board of directors of the local public television station.

In 1971, four years after Bob began his successful practice, he was presented with an incredible opportunity. Sacramento's city council districts had been reformed, and the incumbent city councilman, a politically vulnerable Republican, did not stand a very strong chance for re-election. After discussing the possibilities with friends and family, Bob acted on a long-held dream and decided to run for office. To this day, Bob urges aspiring young Asian American politicians to be aggressive and let their ambitions be known. "I think it's good to say people were coming to me, asking me to run, but the reality is that that's not the way these things happen," he says. "You have to send the signal before people will notice you."

Bob enlisted the help of his parents, his parents' friends, and the support of the larger Asian American community in Sacramento. Working on a shoestring budget of $8,600, he and his supporters walked the precincts of his district and knocked on doors. They made several hundred hand-painted signs. It was the Matsuis' first political experience, and their foresight and perseverance paid off. In California, candidates for city councils who win the majority of

The Matsuis in 1978 with House speaker Tip O'Neill.

the votes in their district in the primary elections do not have to run again in a formal election. There were nine other people in the primary for Sacramento city council. The incumbent received 23% of the vote. Bob, with 54%, scored his first political victory. He served as Sacramento city councilman for seven years. In 1977, his fellow councillors chose him to become vice-mayor.

The following year, another opportunity arrived. Sacramento's representative in the U.S. House of Representatives confided to Bob that he would not run for re-election. Bob saw the chance to finally have a say in policy-making at the national level and decided again to run.

There were three candidates in the primary for the congressional seat—the mayor of Sacramento, a state assemblyman, and Bob Matsui. The first polls in the race were not encouraging. Bob trailed behind the other two candidates with only 6% of the voters supporting him. But in the end he won. In this election as in the election to city council, the deciding factor was the Matsuis' connections to the Asian American community. Even though Asian Americans made up only 6% of the voters in the district, Asian American and other community organizations mobilized to promote Bob's candidacy. "People didn't quite understand that race, and even now don't know how I won," Bob said, "but we just had a much more intense support group."

Once they arrived in Washington, Bob and Doris threw themselves into their work. Since then, Doris has distinguished herself as an activist for women's and children's health, for the arts, and for education. She has been a leader of Peace Links, an international organization that promotes cultural exchange and international goodwill. She has also worked aggressively to promote awareness of breast cancer. As president of the Congressional Club, which is made up of spouses of members of Congress, the White House Cabinet, and the Supreme Court, Doris was the chief sponsor of Project Awareness, which established pilot projects in communities throught the United States to promote the early detection of breast cancer. Project Awareness, working with the YWCA and corporate sponsors, also set up a program to provide mammogram screening for low-income women.

Bob began his junior term in the House of Representatives as a member of the House Judiciary committee. As he vied with other first-term representatives for positions on the most influential House committees, he was confronted with racism. "I said I wanted to be on the anti-trust subcommittee, because I had been practicing law and I did a lot of business work," Bob recalled. "And I was told by the leadership that they would have thought I wanted to serve on the immigration subcommittee." Bob's status as a fourth generation American, not to mention his professional experience, vanished in the shadow of people's perceptions of him as a foreigner.

This initial embarrassment did not prevent Bob from securing a seat on the House Ways and Means Committee. With jurisdiction over tax, trade, health care, social security, and welfare issues, and with enormous influence on national economic policy, the committee is widely considered to be the most powerful one in the House.

After fourteen years in the House, Bob Matsui is now the ranking Democrat on the Ways and Means Subcommittee on Trade and Tariffs and has made a name for himself as a leader in the development of national tax and trade policy.

His performance on behalf of NAFTA left a deep impression on his colleagues. He changed the law to promote mass transit use by offering tax incentives to employers who subsidize the transit expenses of their employees. He also instituted a tax credit for the production of renewable energy sources.

Matsui is also the ranking member of the Ways and Means Subcommittee on Human Resources, which allows him to influence the formation of policy on issues ranging from welfare reform and foster care to employment and disability. In 1993, he worked with children's advocates to secure federal money for programs that were designed to prevent child abuse and neglect and to keep families together. He drafted legislation that became the backbone for child welfare reform, and he has also promoted children's health insurance as a priority in the Ways and Means Committee's deliberations over health care reform.

In 1991, Bob was nominated and elected treasurer of the Democratic National Committee, making him the first Asian American to become an officer of a national political party. In the same year, he was appointed to serve on the House Budget Committee and was also elected to the Democratic Steering and Policy Committee, the leadership panel that selects committee assignments and develops strategy for the House of Representatives.

Bob has remained true to his initial motivations to enter public service, and he has used his power in Congress to act on behalf of Asian American voters and as well as all people of color. Certain political issues are particularly important to Asian Americans. Since Asian Americans own 25% of all small businesses, the community is especially sensitive to fluctuations in the economy, to changes in trade, and to modifications of the tax law. Another subject of concern is hate crime. In the United States, bias-related crime against Asian Americans is on the rise, second only to bias-related crimes targeting gay men and lesbians. Immigration law and bilingual education are also important topics for Asian Americans, 60% of whom were born in Asia.

On all counts, Representative Matsui has spoken out and taken action. Aside from his involvement with tax and trade issues, he was a leading advocate of legislation that mandated the collection and publication of statistics on hate crime. He led the effort to prevent the Census Bureau from lumping all Asian Americans into one category in the 1990 census.

Matsui was also prominent in the fight against the unjust treatment of 2,000 workers, mainly of Filipino, Chinese, and native Alaskan descent, at the Ward's Cove cannery in Alaska. There the workers were paid less than their white coworkers and segregated from them in housing and eating facilities. The Wards Cove cannery spent $2 million in legal fees and $175,000 in lobbying expenses to modify the Civil Rights Act of 1991 in order to exempt the company from having to prove the business necessity of its discriminatory actions. The fight to remove the exemption went all the way to the Senate, but word came back that if the exemption was taken out, President Bush would veto the bill. The Civil Rights Act of 1991 was passed with the language exempting Ward's Cove intact.

The outcome of the Ward's Cove controversy shocked Asian Americans across the country. It demonstrated how callously indifferent American political leadership could be to Asian Americans and to injustices committed against

Doris Matsui with President Bill Clinton during ceremonies celebrating Asian Pacific Heritage Month in May 1993.

them. Ward's Cove galvanized young Asian Americans to get involved in the political process as they never had before.

Before the congressional and presidential elections of 1992, Asian American participation in politics was unusual. Asian Americans have been dismally underrepresented at all levels of government. In addition, voter registration among Asian Americans who are eligible to vote continues to sag. Approximately 30% of Asian Americans vote, compared to 60% of whites. And only 20% of California's 3 million Asian American residents—over a third of the total Asian American population—exercise their right to vote.

Ironically, since the mid-1980s, Asian Americans have been second only to Jewish Americans in the amount of money they have contributed per capita to political campaigns. But it could hardly be said that Asian Americans were getting their money's worth. Despite the dollars the Asian American community gave to President Bush's campaign, he did not appoint any Asian Americans to his cabinet. When he had the opportunity to promote Elaine Chao from Deputy Secretary of Transportation to Secretary of Transportation, he appointed her instead as head of the Peace Corps, a move considered by many to be an insult, tantamount to a demotion.

In response to these indignities, Asian Americans decided to act. In 1992, they were even more active in both Democratic and Republican campaigns than they were in 1988. Moreover, in addition to the reelection campaigns of Bob Matsui and Norman Mineta, three other Asian American candidates, all from California, also ran for seats in the House of Representatives. Although only one of the newcomers was elected, the campaigns clearly signaled the emergence of a new Asian American political consciousness and a new impetus—

especially among younger Asian Americans—to act on their own behalf rather than trust someone else to act for them.

Needless to say, the Matsuis are pleased with these developments. Bob and Doris Matsui, the most visible and outspoken Asian American couple in Washington, are blazing trails for young Asian Americans who want to become involved in the political process.

Bob emphasizes that Asian Americans are still under-represented in government. The few Asian Americans in Congress are already looking for young leaders to take up the torch. Moreover, Asian Americans are needed in all spheres of the political process, not just in public office. "We need more young Asian Americans, men and women, who will become political consultants, who will become pollsters, who will become experts in the political process," he says.

Bob Matsui feels that Asian American political clout will grow when Americans get used to seeing Asian Americans in positions of leadership, speaking out on issues which affect everyone. When he first announced he was running for Congress, some Asian American staffers he knew at the California State Legislature balked. "Bob," they said, "you want to run for Congress?"

In the future as the Matsuis envision it—indeed, as they have helped to fashion it—if their son Brian, now a student at Berkeley, decides to run for public office, no one will even blink.

Architect Ieoh Ming Pei in 1979.

Ieoh

Ming

Pei

IEOH MING PEI OCCUPIES A PLACE IN THE ARCHI-
tectural firmament shared by a precious few. He is an architect
of global stature, the principal designer of nearly fifty projects
around the world, more than half of which have won major
awards. Whether it is a museum, office tower, or concert hall,
a Pei building excites the eye and leaves an indelible impression on the visitor. For the client, whether a corporation, a
university, or a government body, a Pei building is a status
symbol, a mark of taste, prestige, and power. After decades in
the business with many spectacular ups and near-disastrous
downs, I. M. Pei is an icon in the world of architecture, a
towering visionary, and the demand for his work is unceasing.

Pei is the recipient of countless prizes, awards, and
honors. The short speech he gave to accept the 1983 Pritzker
Architecture Prize offers some keys to his philosophy as an
architect. "I believe that architecture is a pragmatic art," Pei
said. "Freedom of expression, for me, consists in moving
within a measured range that I assign to each of my undertak-
ings." He remarked that a building must balance the needs of
the client with those of the community. It must also respect
the surrounding environment. He agreed that modernism, the
school of architecture from which his own style developed,
has given rise to some buildings that are sterile and alienating.
But with a devotion to clean geometric forms and to the use
of the latest technology and materials, modernism has provided an aesthetic for the twentieth century that is coherent
yet flexible, and an architectural style that is responsive to the
values of modern life.

The principle of freedom within discipline has guided
Pei's work. For this reason his style defies easy categorization,
and critics continue to debate whether he is modernist or

postmodernist. He has produced a body of work of astonishing diversity. Nonetheless, his style is instantly recognizable and shows a striking continuity. "You cannot have an architectural revolution every twenty years," he said, "Architecture is not a matter of fashion." Pei's design style shows a love of pure geometric shapes and sleek surfaces. Eventually, he mastered the technique of overlapping shapes. He overlapped triangles for the East Wing of the National Gallery in Washington, D.C., for example, and overlapped ovals for the Meyerson Symphony Hall in Dallas. The technique is part of the visual intrigue that captivates visitors at first sight of a Pei building and grows as they approach and enter. Dramatic entrances, strategically placed windows and openings, the juxtaposition of materials and surfaces, the use of sculpture, the animation of space and light—all contribute to the element of surprise and to the visual excitement that have made his buildings enormously popular with the public.

Unlike architects who approach potential commissions with sketches of preconceived designs, Pei arrives at initial client meetings with nothing. He asks questions, studies the site, and thinks about it. Then he designs. It was this quality that struck Jacqueline Kennedy Onassis back in 1964, when she interviewed a parade of the world's greatest architects in search of someone to design the John F. Kennedy Memorial Library in Boston. "He didn't seem to have just one way to solve a problem," she said. She selected Pei, who was virtually unknown, over the likes of such luminaries as Philip Johnson, Louis Kahn, and Mies van der Rohe. It was the first commission that brought Pei national fame.

In public, Pei is well known for his charm and his salesmanship. Despite the controversy that has surrounded his work, he rarely loses his temper. In private, Pei and his wife avoid the whirlwind of New York's social circuit and prefer small gatherings with close friends who share their love for good food, wine, art, and poetry. Their home on Sutton Place in Manhattan is graced by the works of artists like Jean Dubuffet and Willem de Kooning. The shelves are stacked with books about art.

Pei says that because his training was American, he is essentially an American architect. But one element of his work—the complex and intimate rapport between architecture and nature—can be traced to his childhood days in China. He was born on April 26, 1917, in Guangzhou, formerly Canton, southern China's foremost commercial and industrial city, situated at the head of the Pearl River Delta, northwest of Hong Kong. Ieoh Ming was the second child of Tsuyee Pei, a prosperous banker from a wealthy, landowning family, and of Lien Kwun Pei. Ieoh Ming had an older sister, Yuen Hua, as well as a younger sister, Wei, and two younger brothers, Kwun and Chung.

Ieoh Ming was born during turbulent years in China. Although his family lived comfortably, the country was devastated by famine, and fighting between local warlords threatened to engulf Canton, now known as Guangzhou. The year after he was born, Pei's family left Guangzhou for Hong Kong, where his father became head of that city's branch of the Bank of China. In 1927, Tsuyee Pei was named manager of another bank in the bustling, cosmopolitan port city of Shanghai, and the family moved again.

Ieoh Ming had a traditional relationship with his father. They were respectful of each other but somewhat distant. By contrast, he had a very close relationship with his mother, who was a talented musician and a faithful Buddhist. Ieoh Ming was singled out among his siblings for the special privilege of accompanying her on religious retreats in the countryside. She died after a long illness when Ieoh Ming was only thirteen. He was never able to become as intimate with his stepmother, whom his father married three years later.

While working in Shanghai, Pei's father maintained a house in Suzhou, a small city northwest of Shanghai where Peis have lived for generations. Positioned between major cities on the Grand Canal, Suzhou grew wealthy from the trade of silk and rice. Its prosperous residents commissioned the best artists and craftsworkers to build and decorate their homes and gardens.

The Pei retreat was called the Garden of the Lion Forest. In the Lion Forest, picture windows and passageways brought the house and the garden together in an intricate fashion. Wherever Ieoh Ming found himself in the house, he was never far away from nature. The Garden of the Lion Forest, where architecture and nature were inseparable, made an indelible impression on him, and later it would exert a profound influence on his sensibilities as an architect.

Pei went to Saint John's Middle School in Shanghai, which was run by Protestant missionaries and attended by many of the sons of Shanghai's elite. Afterward, Tsuyee, who had acquired numerous business contacts with foreigners, wanted Ieoh Ming to go to college in England. But the teenager was captivated by American culture as it was portrayed in the movies. Across the street from the movie theater in Shanghai where he got his first taste of Americana, the Park Hotel was undergoing construction. The sight of the twenty-three-story building, the tallest building in Shanghai, captured

Ieoh Ming's imagination. Later on in his career, he said that the Park Hotel first sparked his interest in architecture.

Ieoh Ming consented to his father's wishes to take the entrance examinations for Oxford, but on the condition that if he passed, he could choose for himself which college he would attend. He passed the entrance exams but then announced his intention to study not at Oxford but at the University of Pennsylvania in Philadelphia, for a degree in architecture.

Pei traveled to the United States by boat. He arrived in San Francisco, and from there he took a train to Philadelphia. His experience at the University of Pennsylvania, where he enrolled in the fall of 1934, was discouraging. He was intimidated by his classmates' superior abilities at drawing, a skill in which he felt sorely inadequate. Moreover, the architecture program at Penn was disappointingly conventional, with an emphasis on the Beaux Arts, a school of architecture

I. M. Pei in his New York office in 1981.

that imitated the designs of ancient Greek and Roman monu-
ments. It was especially popular in the United States after the
turn of the century, when the young nation, rich with the
accumulated wealth of the industrial revolution, sought an
architectural style that would match that of the greatest
capitals of Europe and signal America's emergence as a growing world power. But after the First World War, the style had
become cliché. In the meantime, European architects had
moved on to more daring and exciting innovations.

In the fall of 1935, Pei, having given up his aspirations
of becoming an architect, transferred to the Massachusetts
Institute of Technology in Cambridge to study engineering.
However, William Emerson, dean of the architecture school,
recognized Pei's talent and tried to persuade him to return to
architecture. The architecture school at MIT, like Penn, was
also rooted in the Beaux Arts style. But in the MIT library,
Pei read about new trends in Europe where architectural
design had taken a radical turn, and where young architects,
repudiating the Beaux Arts school, were designing simple
buildings of pure form, entirely stripped of ornament. Pei
graduated from MIT with a bachelor's degree in architecture
in 1940, but it wasn't until he went to graduate school that
his identity as an architect began to take shape. The knowledge of science and technology that he acquired at MIT would
prove to be of enormous value to him later in his career.

While he was at MIT, Pei had a chance meeting that
changed his life. Eileen Loo, a young woman who left China
in 1938 to study at Wellesley College, stopped in New York
on her way to Boston. On the train she met one of Pei's MIT
fraternity brothers. When they arrived at Grand Central, he
introduced Eileen to Pei, who offered to drive her the rest of

the way to Boston. Since Eileen already had a train ticket, she politely refused. Nonetheless, he called her later for a date.

Pei had planned to return home after graduation. But the Japanese had invaded China, and his father warned him to remain in the United States. In the meantime, his relationship with Eileen grew. After she graduated from Wellesley in 1942, they married. The following fall, Eileen enrolled in the landscape-architecture program at Harvard. Eileen's studies at Harvard exposed Pei to Harvard's architecture department, which was fast earning a reputation for its progressive philosophy and its avant-garde curriculum. The architecture department at Harvard was headed by Walter Gropius, who had founded the Bauhaus in Germany in 1919.

The Bauhaus was the most important school of modern design in Europe until the Nazis closed it in 1933. The Bauhaus curriculum was innovative, fusing the study of arts and crafts. In 1927, architecture was added to the curriculum. The Bauhaus valued technology and emphasized the use of the latest materials and techniques. Modernists from the Bauhaus sought to improve not just architecture but the quality of life by making buildings that were efficient and modern.

Gropius and Marcel Breuer brought the principles of modernist design to Harvard when they arrived in 1937. For Pei, the department, with its adventurous ideas and its idealistic spirit, was an exciting place to study and work, and its influence on his sensibilities as an architect was immeasurable. "I want a young architect to find his way in whatever circumstances," Gropius wrote in the *Architectural Record*, "I want him independently to create true, genuine forms out of the technical, economic, and social conditions in which he finds

himself instead of imposing a learned formula onto the surroundings."

Pei enrolled in Harvard's Graduate School of Design
in December 1942. But the following month, he took time
off to volunteer at the National Defense Research Committee
in Princeton, New Jersey, where he helped to plan the bombing of bridges in Germany and Italy, and later the bombing
of cities in Japan. In the summer of 1945, Eileen gave birth
to their first child, Ting Chung. Eileen gave up her studies at
Harvard to care for him. Ting Chung was followed by two
more sons, Chien Chung and Li Chung, and a daughter, Liane.
(Chien Chung and Li Chung are now architects for Pei, Cobb,
Freed & Associates.)

In the fall of 1945, Pei returned to Harvard to study
and teach, for he was offered a post as an assistant professor.
The students and faculty enjoyed an unusual closeness, spending many hours at bars around campus talking about their
work. He and Eileen managed to enjoy themselves on a modest
budget, spending their money on records and wine.

Despite the modernist ideals that prevailed at Harvard, Pei had his own ideas and opinions. He felt that buildings of the future could preserve the best elements of the past
without the slavish imitation of external details practiced by
the school of Beaux Arts. To prove his point, he presented a
plan for an art museum for Shanghai. It was the first of several
challenges Pei accepted throughout his career to fuse his
architectural ideas with the influence of his Chinese heritage.
"My problem is to find an architectural expression that will
be truly Chinese without any resort to Chinese architectural
details and motives as we know them," he said. Pei isolated
two elements of Chinese architecture, the bare wall and the

garden patio, and successfully worked them into his plan for the museum. "All forms of Chinese art are directly or indirectly results of a sensitive observation of nature," he remarked to the journal *Progressive Architecture.* Pei's plan synthesized modernism's clean geometry and efficient use of space with a sensitivity to natural surroundings, successfully bringing art and nature together.

In 1948, while he was still an assistant professor at Harvard, Pei met William Zeckendorf, a flamboyant New York real estate developer. At the pinnacle of his career, Zeckendorf ran an empire of hotels and office and apartment buildings worth hundreds of millions of dollars. What distinguished him from other real estate developers was his love of architecture. He sought to enhance the prestige of his development ventures with high-quality design, and to do this he wanted to set up an in-house design staff for his firm, Webb & Knapp.

Zeckendorf had asked a friend at the Museum of Modern Art to scout young architects. After screening a dozen, he recommended the 31-year-old Pei. Zeckendorf was impressed with the young man. Aside from Pei's cordial affability, the two shared a taste in good food and wine. At first Pei hesitated about leaving his teaching post at Harvard, and he still intended to return to China. But he was interested in playing a part in Zeckendorf's ambitious plans. In the fall, he became director of Webb & Knapp's architecture division. Eileen closed up the apartment in Cambridge and the family moved to New York.

During his years at Webb & Knapp, Pei gained valuable experience. As director of the architecture division, he sought commissions and oversaw the design and construction

was the John F. Kennedy Library in Boston (1965–79). The library, which was to house a collection of Kennedy memorabilia, was first slated to be built on the campus of Harvard. Local resistance to the potential tourist trap, and the continuous stalling of the project by city officials, made the library a time-consuming and frustrating project for Pei to complete. The library finally opened at its new site in Dorchester, Massachusetts, on the bank of the Charles River, to mixed reviews. But it was his first major use of a massive glass atrium, which became one of his signature design elements. It warmed the interior and opened the space to the various moods of the sky.

Pei's reputation was nearly ruined with the construction of the John Hancock Building in Boston (1966–76). The slender glass tower became the object of derision and scandal when its windows began to fall out. Later it was established that the error had been committed by the glass company, and the windows were eventually replaced. Nevertheless, the disaster nearly ended Pei's career.

With the commission to build the East Wing of the National Gallery of Art in Washington, D.C., the Pei firm had the chance to redeem itself. The resulting product, a marble and glass structure composed of interlocking triangular forms, was a resounding success with the critics and the public when it opened in 1978. "People love the East Building; they take joy in its energy, in its light, in its sense of movement," remarked Paul Goldberger in the *New York Times* a decade after the East Wing opened. "In the end, the East Building serves . . . as a kind of celebration of architecture—an advertisement for the pleasures of architecture and, by extension, the pleasures of art."

Pei's work also brought a long-awaited if tenuous reunion with his homeland. In 1974, he returned to China for a visit, his first in nearly forty years. He was invited again for two visits in 1978 to discuss plans for a commission. Pei was horrified by the government's original proposal to build a skyscraper hotel in Beijing, just outside the low-lying Forbidden City. He first convinced the government to ban high-rises within sight of the Forbidden City. Then he convinced them to commission instead a low-lying hotel complex in a mountainous, wooded area outside of the city.

For the Fragrant Hill Hotel (1979–1982), Pei was again challenged to find a design that was both Chinese and modern. He utilized bare walls, garden patios, and picture windows overlooking the hotel's natural surroundings, which had once been an imperial hunting preserve. Pei designed ornamentation for the walls, provoking critics to say that Pei had finally succumbed to postmodernist impulses. Shoddy workmanship, inferior materials, and bureaucratic complications stalled the opening of the hotel. Nonetheless, Pei's design succeeded, as it intended, in bringing human living space and nature together.

Even though Pei left China at the age of 17, he continued to have strong feelings for his homeland. He used the $100,000 award that accompanied the Pritzker Architecture Prize to set up a fellowship to allow Chinese architecture students to study in the United States. In 1989, massive student demonstrations were organized in Beijing to protest government corruption and to demand political reform. The government of China ordered the military to crack down on the protests; tanks were brought to Tiananmen Square, and the ensuing violence resulted in bloodshed and many deaths.

Pei communicated his shock and his deep sadness in an editorial that was published in the *New York Times.* "We saw a new generation of young men and women, less scarred by the terrible history of the country, coming into their own," he wrote. "We wanted to believe that a more open and modern China was possible." The tragedy had occurred just as he and Eileen realized their long-held dreams of working in China again. It shattered their hopes that the country's leadership, like its youth, was finally opening to new ideas. "Will we ever be able to work in China again?" he asked. "I am not sure."

The late 1980s were great years for Pei, marked by a succession of architectural triumphs. In 1988, the Jacob Javits Convention Center opened in New York City, a vast, multi-tiered glass atrium spanning five city blocks. This was followed, in 1989, by the openings of the Morton Meyerson Symphony Center, a uniquely sensuous work of marble and glass, in Dallas, Texas, and of the seventy-story Bank of China tower in Hong Kong.

The same year marked the inauguration of Pei's pyramid extension of the Louvre—perhaps the most dangerous commission Pei had ever accepted. The Louvre is home to the most famous collection of art in the world. It is an international landmark and a French national treasure. But before the expansion, the building suffered from several serious structural problems. At first sight of the sprawling museum, the question visitors most frequently asked was: Where is the entrance? There was also a severe shortage of exhibition and storage spaces. The thousands of daily visitors were serviced by only two restrooms and an inadequate cafeteria. To get from one part of the museum to another, visitors had to trudge through its entire length, since the expansive outdoor space between the museum's wings was filled with a dingy, unflattering parking lot. By the late 1970s, France's hallowed landmark was all but ignored by the French themselves. A survey in 1977 found that only 30% of the visitors to the Louvre were French, and only 10% were Parisian.

In September 1981, French president François Mitterand decided to initiate a series of improvements that would restore the Louvre to its former glory. This included ejecting the government's Ministry of Finance from the north wing of the Louvre, as well as commissioning a large-scale renovation and expansion of the museum. Instead of holding a competition for an architect, the usual procedure for such a huge civic project, Mitterand consulted Emile Basiani, who later became president of the government agency set up to improve the Louvre. Basiani spent nine months touring museums in Europe and the United States. The East Wing of the National Gallery made a striking impression on him, and he recommended to President Mitterand that Pei be selected for the renovation of the Louvre.

When Basiani first approached Pei with the commission, Pei hesitated. He said that it was "probably impossible" to alter the Louvre. But after three trips to Paris, three months of studying the history of the museum and analyzing its current problems, Pei decided that improvement was not only necessary but feasible. He called Basiani with a solution.

What the Louvre needed most was space—for storage and restoration, for restrooms, restaurants, and information centers, and for parking. Pei proposed excavating the Cour Napoléon and building a complex for all these facilities

*In Paris in 1989,
Pei stands before the
controversial glass and
steel pyramid he
designed as part of a
major renovation
of the Louvre.*

underground. Such a complex would also link the wings of
the Louvre, reducing the time it took to go from one wing to
another.

What the Louvre also needed was an entrance. Pei
felt that the museum was so vast that visitors needed an
obvious focal point, the best location for which, he believed,
was the Cour Napoléon. The entrance had to be a striking
structure that would be instantly recognizable without upstag-
ing the museum. Pei proposed that the parking lot be removed
from the Cour Napoléon, and that a great plaza be built in its
place, with a sleek pyramid at its center. Because the pyramid

would be transparent and two-thirds the height of the Louvre, it would not block the view of the museum's ornate facade, reflections of which would be caught in pools of water surrounding the pyramid.

At this point in his career, Pei was well acquainted with controversy. Because his commissions had always been monumental in scale and importance, preparation for political battle had always been an important part of his thought process. Pei's ease with the wealthy and powerful has not only been a boon, but a necessity, for his experience has shown the value of clients who can also act as influential political allies.

Pei was accustomed to the press and the public balking at his astronomical budgets. Because of the materials, the techniques, and the workmanship required, Pei buildings are very costly to construct. The expansion and renovation of the Louvre cost over six billion francs, the equivalent of over a billion dollars. But in the case of the Louvre, something much more precious than money was at stake, for Pei's client was not President Mitterand, but the whole of France.

Pei was little prepared for the fury of the attack that greeted his proposal for the Louvre. Mitterand's opponents in the French government denounced the pyramid project and called Mitterand's failure to seek outside approval in the selection of an architect an outright act of tyranny. Architecture critics howled about the prospect of another eyesore in the heart of Paris, for modern architecture did not have a good track record in the city. Some critics, insidiously xenophobic in tone, belittled the commission as an Egyptian-inspired monument by an American architect, or worse yet, an architect who was not even American, but Chinese. Critics called the pyramid proposal an "atrocity," "The House of the Dead," and "an annex to Disneyland." A poll found that while 90% of the French supported renovation of the Louvre, only 10% approved of the pyramid. An antipyramid lobby even succeeded in enlisting 15,000 members. Nevertheless, the lobby failed to secure support among France's leading cultural figures, several of whom were outspoken in their support of the pyramid.

Jacques Chirac, the mayor of Paris, demanded that a mock pyramid of the proposed dimensions be erected at the site. For several days in the spring of 1985, a crane held cables aloft, indicating the size and shape of the pyramid, and thousands of curious Parisians came to look. Slowly the tide of public opinion began to turn. When the pyramid complex opened in 1989, followed by the renovated north wing in the fall of 1993, both received stunning critical and popular acclaim.

In November 1993, at the conclusion of a press conference held for the debut of the north wing, the director of the museum, Michel Laclotte, announced that Pei had to leave. He asked if there were any more questions for the architect. Someone in the back of the room simply cried, "Merci!" (Thank-you). In a rare show of enthusiasm, the French press, bitter enemies of Pei's proposal a decade earlier, warmly applauded Pei as he exited. It was in many ways the culmination of the trials and triumphs of his career. "It was the most important project of my life," Pei said after the opening. "I hope to do many more things, but never again will I have another opportunity like the Louvre."

At the age of 72, after forty years as the head of I. M. Pei & Associates, rumors circulated that Pei, having reached the summit of his profession, was going to retire. Instead he decided to scale down his role. The firm was renamed Pei, Cobb, Freed & Associates to acknowledge the contributions his partners had made to the success of the firm, and to signal that responsibilities at the firm were shifting. The decision freed him to pursue the kind of design work he was never able to accept as the director of a staff of 350 people. This has included an expansion of the Mount Sinai Medical Center in New York, a belltower in Japan, museums in Luxembourg and Paris, and office towers in Spain.

When a journalist asked Pei what he would like to design to close his long career, he gave a deceptively simple, deeply personal answer. "A house perhaps," he said, "A house for my wife and me. But the simplicity [of it] is among the most difficult things in the world. I'm not able to do it yet. In two or three years, perhaps."

Further Reading

Chan, Sucheng. *Asian Americans: An Interpretive History.*
Boston: Twayne, 1991.

Gee, Emma, ed. *Asian Women.* Berkeley: Asian American
Studies, University of California, 1971.

Golub, Caroline. *Immigrant Destinations.* Philadelphia:
Temple University Press, 1977.

Kitano, Harry H. L., and Roger Daniels. *Asian Americans:
Emerging Minorities.* Englewood Cliffs, NJ: Prentice Hall,
1988.

Perrin, Linda. *Coming to America: Immigrants from the Far East.*
New York: Delacorte, 1980.

Reimers, David M. *The Immigrant Experience.* New York:
Chelsea House, 1989.

Tachiki, Amy, ed. *Roots: An Asian American Reader.* Los
Angeles: UCLA Asian American Studies Center, 1971.

Takaki, Ronald. *From Different Shores: Perspectives on Race
and Ethnicity in America.* New York: Oxford University
Press, 1987.

———. *Strangers from a Different Shore: A History of Asian
Americans.* Boston: Little, Brown, 1989.

Index

Picture Credits

AP/Wide World Photos: pp. 14, 16, 21, 26, 35, 39, 41, 44, 46, 49, 52, 54, 82, 87, 103, 106, 115, 118, 123, 129, 134; The Bettmann Archive: p. 36; Don Hamerman photo: p. 59; Nanine Hartzenbusch, © 1993 *New York Newsday:* p. 63; Courtesy Dr. David Ho: pp. 56, 61; Courtesy Loida Nicolas Lewis: p. 91; Courtesy of Office of Congressman Robert T. Matsui: p. 112; Office of Congressman Norman Mineta: pp. 76, 79; Courtesy Josie Cruz Natori: pp. 66, 69, 71, 74; Public Information Office, University of California: pp. 94 (John Blaustein photo), 98; Jane Scherr: p. 100; © Sirlin Photographers, Sacramento, CA: p. 108; TLC Beatrice International: pp. 84 (Ira Bloch photo), 88; UPI/Bettmann: pp. 6, 10, 13, 80; White House Photo Department: p. 115.

RONALD TAKAKI, the son of immigrant plantation laborers from Japan, graduated from the College of Wooster, Ohio, and earned his Ph.D. in history from the University of California at Berkeley, where he has served both as the chairperson and the graduate adviser of the Ethnic Studies program. Professor Takaki has lectured widely on issues relating to ethnic studies and multiculturalism in the United States, Japan, and the former Soviet Union and has won several important awards for his teaching efforts. He is the author of six books, including the highly acclaimed *Strangers from a Different Shore: A History of Asian Americans*, and the recently published *A Different Mirror: A History of Multicultural America*.

ANGELO RAGAZA is the managing editor of *A. Magazine*. Born in Los Angeles, he graduated from Columbia University with a degree in French studies. He currently lives in New York City.